The law relating to the child : its protection, education, and employment : with an introduction on the laws of Spain, Germany, France, and Italy and bibliography.

Robert Wolstenholme Holland

The law relating to the child : its protection, education, and employment : with an introduction on the laws of Spain, Germany, France, and Italy and bibliography.
Holland, Robert Wolstenholme
collection ID CTRG97-B1460
Reproduction from York University Law School Library
Publisher's advertising including in paging. Includes index.
London ; New York : Sir I. Pitman & Sons, [1914].
xxiv, 142, 16 p. ; 22 cm

The Making of Modern Law collection of legal archives constitutes a genuine revolution in historical legal research because it opens up a wealth of rare and previously inaccessible sources in legal, constitutional, administrative, political, cultural, intellectual, and social history. This unique collection consists of three extensive archives that provide insight into more than 300 years of American and British history. These collections include:

Legal Treatises, 1800-1926: over 20,000 legal treatises provide a comprehensive collection in legal history, business and economics, politics and government.

Trials, 1600-1926: nearly 10,000 titles reveal the drama of famous, infamous, and obscure courtroom cases in America and the British Empire across three centuries.

Primary Sources, 1620-1926: includes reports, statutes and regulations in American history, including early state codes, municipal ordinances, constitutional conventions and compilations, and law dictionaries.

These archives provide a unique research tool for tracking the development of our modern legal system and how it has affected our culture, government, business – nearly every aspect of our everyday life. For the first time, these high-quality digital scans of original works are available via print-on-demand, making them readily accessible to libraries, students, independent scholars, and readers of all ages.

bibliolife
old books, new life.

The BiblioLife Network

This project was made possible in part by the BiblioLife Network (BLN), a project aimed at addressing some of the huge challenges facing book preservationists around the world. The BLN includes libraries, library networks, archives, subject matter experts, online communities and library service providers. We believe every book ever published should be available as a high-quality print reproduction; printed on-demand anywhere in the world. This insures the ongoing accessibility of the content and helps generate sustainable revenue for the libraries and organizations that work to preserve these important materials.

The following book is in the "public domain" and represents an authentic reproduction of the text as printed by the original publisher. While we have attempted to accurately maintain the integrity of the original work, there are sometimes problems with the original work or the micro-film from which the books were digitized. This can result in minor errors in reproduction. Possible imperfections include missing and blurred pages, poor pictures, markings and other reproduction issues beyond our control. Because this work is culturally important, we have made it available as part of our commitment to protecting, preserving, and promoting the world's literature.

GUIDE TO FOLD-OUTS MAPS and OVERSIZED IMAGES

The book you are reading was digitized from microfilm captured over the past thirty to forty years. Years after the creation of the original microfilm, the book was converted to digital files and made available in an online database.

In an online database, page images do not need to conform to the size restrictions found in a printed book. When converting these images back into a printed bound book, the page sizes are standardized in ways that maintain the detail of the original. For large images, such as fold-out maps, the original page image is split into two or more pages

Guidelines used to determine how to split the page image follows:

- Some images are split vertically; large images require vertical and horizontal splits.
- For horizontal splits, the content is split left to right.
- For vertical splits, the content is split from top to bottom.
- For both vertical and horizontal splits, the image is processed from top left to bottom right.

LAW LIBRARY

YORK UNIVERSITY

THE LAW RELATING TO
THE CHILD
ITS

PROTECTION, EDUCATION,

AND EMPLOYMENT

With Introduction on the Laws of
SPAIN, GERMANY, FRANCE, and ITALY
and Bibliography

BY

ROBERT WOLSTENHOLME HOLLAND,
M.A., M.Sc., LL.D.
SOMETIME DAUNTESLY LEGAL SCHOLAR OF THE MANCHESTER
UNIVERSITY, OF THE MIDDLE TEMPLE, BARRISTER-AT-LAW

LONDON
SIR ISAAC PITMAN & SONS, LTD., 1 AMEN CORNER, E.C.
BATH, NEW YORK AND MELBOURNE

1914

Printed by Sir Isaac Pitman
& Sons, Ltd., London, Bath,
New York and Melbourne

CONTENTS

INTRODUCTION

CHAP.		PAGE
	THE LAWS OF SPAIN, GERMANY, FRANCE, AND ITALY ON THIS SUBJECT, INCLUDING BIBLIOGRAPHY OF ITALIAN LITERATURE	V

BIBLIOGRAPHY

	OF GERMAN, FRENCH, AND ENGLISH LITERATURE	XIX
	TABLE OF CASES	XXIII
I.	THE PROTECTION OF CHILDREN: THEIR MORAL WELFARE	1
II.	THE PROTECTION OF CHILDREN: THEIR PHYSICAL WELFARE	15
III	INFANT LIFE PROTECTION AND MISCELLANEOUS MATTERS	38
IV	CUSTODY AND MAINTENANCE OF INFANTS	50
V.	RELIGIOUS EDUCATION	60
VI	SECULAR EDUCATION	65
VII	THE EDUCATION OF CHILDREN SUFFERING FROM PHYSICAL AND MENTAL DEFECTS	82
VIII	EDUCATION AND THE PREVENTION AND PUNISHMENT OF CRIME	90
IX.	RESTRICTIONS ON THE EMPLOYMENT OF CHILDREN AND YOUNG PERSONS	116
	INDEX	137

INTRODUCTION

AT the present time, in England, although much good has been done in the way of social legislation for the amelioration of the lot of children, something still remains to bring together the loose ends which have been created by the various Acts of Parliament affecting children's education, birth notification, school feeding, the exploitation of children in industry, their exclusion from public houses, and special Courts for the trial of childish offences. All these matters, so necessarily aimed at the protection of child life, should be gathered together under one central authority, and it is as important that there should be a Minister for the Protection of Childhood as that there should be a Minister for Commerce The failure of social legislation for the betterment of the masses in the past has been in the fact that it has been approached from the wrong end. Even to-day there seems to be no provision made for the case of the child who has passed beyond the stage of being an infant in arms, but has not yet come to the minimum age for receiving elementary education (*i e*, the age of five years) Several European countries are ahead of us in this respect, Germany and Belgium in particular having made provision in kindergartens for this purpose. In France, for children between the ages of two and six, experimental *Ecoles Maternelles* are provided, whilst for children under two the State is experimenting in the provision of *crèches*

The idea of various continental countries that child life should be conserved is based on very different foundations. The essentially military spirit of most of these countries of necessity requires that the physique of the male portion of the population should be kept up In England this has not been the case, but in France and Germany military necessity has not been ignored. Spain, often spoken of as one of the most backward of the civilised countries of Europe, has as long ago as 1878 made provision for the protection of child life, but the object of such provision is clearly seen when the fact is noticed that the Minister of War is in most cases the person responsible for the promulgation of regulations and the carrying out of the law in this respect. Many of the laws of Spain are equal and in some respects superior to the English law in relation to the employment of children. It is only recently in England that the age of sixteen has been laid down as the minimum age at which persons are allowed in subterranean workings; but this has been the law in Spain since 1900. There is in Spain, however, provision made for cases where the law cannot be observed, whilst in England the law must be observed. The excellence of the Spanish laws, so far as they go, cannot be disputed, but in their administration they are extremely doubtful, as it is often found necessary, after the promulgation of the law, to issue further decrees from time to time, setting out the same specific enactments, with or without further explanation. Thus the law of the 13th March, 1900, which contains many of the provisions relating to the employment of children, is practically repeated in the decree of the Minister of War in March, 1902.

The following outline of the provisions of the Spanish law deserves careful comparison with the English law as stated in the ensuing pages.

The minimum working age under the law of 13th March, 1900, is ten years, except where permission is granted for work to commence one year earlier by reason that the particular child is proficient in reading and writing.

Between the ages of ten and fourteen the hours of labour are limited. In factories and purely industrial occupations six hours is the limit for the day's work, whilst the eight hours day is the maximum in offices and commercial life. Here again the *juntas* may allow an extension of these times where, through drought, water mills have been stopped and overtime is necessary, and in the case of factories having steam power any forced stoppage can be made up by increasing the hours of labour.

Education from Ten to Fourteen.

By the law of March, 1900, all children between the ages of ten and fourteen must be allowed two hours daily for primary and religious instruction. They must attend school for this purpose if there is a recognised school within a distance of two kilometres. Where there is no such school, any establishment in which more than twenty children are employed must provide its own school.

If failure is made in this respect the Minister of War may, under a decree of 1902, establish such school

Education to Eighteen.

By regulations issued in May, 1900, it is provided that the master is to concede one hour daily for primary education to all his work-people under eighteen years of age.

If there is no properly equipped school within two kilometres, any establishment employing more than 150 persons must equip in such establishment a school under a competent master. In such school, reading, writing, the elements of Spanish grammar, the first four rules of arithmetic, and Christian doctrine must be taught.

Groups of factories can join in providing schools, and all schools are under the local authorities—Municipal and Provincial *Juntas* —who appoint local inspectors The inspectors report to the local authority, the local authority to the Governor of the Province, the Governor to the Rector of the University in the district, and this latter official compiles statistics for use of the Government

Night Work.

No night work is allowed for children under the age of fourteen, and only in certain industries will persons between fourteen and eighteen be allowed to work at night The selection of industries is left with the local authorities. Work on Sundays and festivals is also restricted

The night is deemed to last from 7 p m to 5 a m, and where persons under eighteen do work in the night, no spell of work must exceed four hours without rest periods of at least one and a half hours The total amount of night work allowed per week by the law of March, 1900, is forty-eight hours, but this appears to have been increased to sixty-six by a decree of 1902

Mining.

Like our law regulating the employment of children in mines, it is laid down that working in mines is restricted to persons over sixteen "Mines" includes mines, tunnels, and surface works where ordinary operations similar to those of mining are carried on

And Other Dangerous Work.

Similar provision is made against persons under sixteen working at employments where inflammable or insalubrious materials are used, and against such persons being engaged in cleaning machinery whilst in motion

Dangerous Performances.

Of like nature to our Dangerous Performances Acts are the provisions against persons under sixteen being engaged in tasks of *agilidad, equilibrio, fuerzo,* etc.

Morals.

The moral protection of persons under sixteen and women under age is the provision that such persons shall not be engaged in printing works where books, pictures, or documents, not coming within the penal law and yet likely to injure the morals, are produced.

Punishment.

The first important laws for protection of children in Spain were promulgated on the 26th July, 1878, and the punishments for infractions of the law are there laid down. In addition, fines have been fixed for breaches of Factory laws

Workman.

By a decree of the Minister of War in March, 1902, a workman is defined as a person who works with pay or without, outside his own home. By the same decree rules for admission of minors to business are laid down

1. Permission of the father, or in default, the mother, or where the child is brought up in a home, the permission of the director of the establishment in which the child had been *asilado* must be obtained

2. His age must be proved by entry on the civil register (*i e*, by certificate of birth).

3. Proof must be forthcoming that the class of work to which the minor is going is not above his strength

4. And that the person is free from any infectious or contagious disease. This is proved by a medical certificate

This brief *résumé* of the Laws of Spain as they affect children illustrates the position in the southern countries of Europe

German Law.

Germany and France, ever to the front in matters of social reform, have each made serious attempts to deal with this problem

It would be a giant task to go into the details of the legislation of these countries. It is only possible here to indicate that the lines along which both countries have advanced are very similar to those followed in England. In addition to this, a bibliography of the works on social legislation and legal principles will sufficiently indicate the point of view adopted in both countries. The literature of Great Britain is extremely weak in this respect.

The most valuable of the condensed literature on the protection of children in Germany is a pamphlet entitled *Der strafrechtliche Schutz des Kindes*—Inaugural = Dissertation zur Erlangung der Doktorwurde der Hohen Juristischen Fakultat der Ruprecht = Karls = Universitat zu Heidelberg vorgelegt von Anna Schultz, which well repays perusal.

The chief provisions of the law in Germany are to be found in the Trade Regulations and in the Law for the Protection of Children of the 30th March, 1903. Hence the important literature of Germany will be that of the last ten years.

The school-leaving age of fourteen is the same as in England, and certain circumstances are laid down under which a child of thirteen may be released from school. In such cases he may not be employed in a factory for more than six hours per day. The daily period is raised, however, to ten hours for children between fourteen and sixteen years of age.

Just as our Mines Regulations Act, 1911, provides for the keeping of an employment register in respect of juvenile employees, so the German law provides for such a book being kept by *all* employers employing persons under age. This book is open to the inspection of the civil authority, but it does not affect domestic servants and children employed in the home.

By the law of 30th March, 1903, the hours of labour and the intervals for rest and refreshment are laid down. Further provision is made for cases of industries (as in Spain) where persons under age should not be employed for moral or hygienic reasons. Moral reasons have not influenced the English legislature to any great extent, but the prohibition against children under sixteen working in mines is an example of a limitation in English law based on hygienic reasons.

German law is rather deficient in the fact that penalties are not exacted from persons who endanger the development of the body, intellect or morality of persons under age. English law is much more satisfactory in this respect. The Criminal Code of Germany does provide against the offence of "ejectment" or abandonment or exposure of children. The punishment is three months' imprisonment for the "ejectment" of youthful persons or invalids by strangers, but six months is the minimum if the parent is responsible for the offence.

French Law.

Having briefly examined the law of Spain as it relates to children, with a view to showing the tendency even in backward countries, and having referred to that of Germany, we may now direct attention to the attitude of France to this matter.

Although the legal status of the child has always been an important matter in France, yet the law which gave birth to the series of laws having for their object the protection of the child was the law of the 24th of July, 1889, " sur la protection des enfants maltraités et moralement abandonnés " Side by side with this law are others falling into three groups governing the labour and education, the protection from harm, and the reclaiming of the juvenile criminal. The law of the 7th December, 1874, relative to the protection of children employed in " les professions ambulantes " was followed by the law of 2nd November, 1892, modified and completed by the law of 30th March, 1900, governing the working of infants, young girls and women in industrial establishments. These laws have been followed quite recently by another regulating the night work of children. The work in this branch is not yet completed, as a number of projected laws are at present before Parliament to limit the employment of children in glass-works and foundries. (Projet de loi sur le travail des enfants dans les usines à feu continu et projet de loi sur l'emploi des enfants dans les verreries)

As in England private enterprise of the charitably inclined has accompanied and sometimes anticipated legislation. The law often works hand in hand with private initiative; thus the law of the 19th April, 1898, recognises private charitable institutions by authorising the juge d'instruction on the Tribunal de l'Enfant to remand a child, guilty under this law " pour la répression des violences " of acts of cruelty, violence, or assault, or against whom such acts are committed, to charitable institutions similar to our industrial schools

Mr. W. L. George, writing in 1908 of France in the twentieth century, says of the Frenchman—

"From childhood upwards he is overworked, and thrives under the burden ; long hours and short holidays are willingly accepted by the people for their children. The law fixes 9½ hours (now 8 since 1912) as the legal working day in factories, a high limit. . . . Moreover the average is counted over six days, for the half-day has not yet entered into national customs. Indeed, up to four or five years ago no child had more than one half-holiday in every week."

This is now changed, and the position of the child is becoming stronger. Up to the age of thirteen, education in France is compulsory, and has reached the masses without any great difficulty.

A problem that has always interested the French lawyer who is naturally a student of philosophy and sociology is the problem of juvenile criminality. The history of legislation in France on this aspect of law is the history of the whole law as to infancy, and it has culminated in the law of the 22nd July, 1912, which came into force on the 4th March, 1914.

This new legislation is for the most part based on similar laws in force in the United States of America, but M. Henri Robert, bâtonnier de l'ordre des avocats, says of it—

"Si certaine qu'ait été sur la nouvelle loi l'influence des institutions américaines, on ne peut pas dire cependant qu'elle soit sortie uniquement des législations étrangères. Par la haute pensée sociale dont elle se réclame, par les principes d'amendement et de relèvement qu'elle consacre, elle est comme l'aboutissement d'une évolution progressive de tout le droit français relatif à l'enfance."

Although in England the idea of children's courts and children's punishments is of recent growth, M. Robert dates the legislation in France to the Penal Code of 1791, in which the question of understanding in relation to criminal offences is expressly noted. Having regard to the fact that the Roman law is the basis of the Code, the old Law of France was inclined to follow the Civil law in this matter, and attempted to mark out in sections a young person's life according to the degree of intelligence expected at various ages to a much finer extent than in English law. The Penal Code of 1791 provided—

"Lorsqu'un accusé déclaré coupable par le jury, 'lit-on au titre

V,' aura commis le crime pour lequel il est poursuivi avant l'âge de seize ans accomplis, les jurés décideront dans les formes ordinaires de leurs délibérations la question suivante : le coupable a-t-il commis le crime avec ou sans discernement ? "

Where the answer was a negative, the child was acquitted and handed to his parents or required " d'être conduit dans une maison de correction pour y être detenu et élevé pendant un certain nombre d'années que le jugement déterminera et qui toutefois ne pourra excéder l'époque à laquelle il aura atteint l'âge de vingt ans." This in France in 1791 was in spirit if not in truth very similar to our present reformatory laws

The Penal Code of 1810 closely followed that of 1791, but unfortunately the " house of correction " did not exist, and in order to comply with the law the departmental prison was called a house of correction for this purpose, and the result was that those who had and those who had no discernment were in the same building and slept in the same rooms, but the former were in prison and the latter in a " house of correction "

The next movement was made by the law of the 5th August, 1850, which had in view the reclaiming of the juvenile criminal and the making of a useful citizen " Colonies pénitentiaires " were founded often in the country where the child found a trade to his hands, and where he was out of contact with other criminals From time to time changes have taken place An inquiry into " pénitentiaires " was made in 1872 and improvements followed The law of the 11th April, 1906, raised the " penal majority " to eighteen years, and finally the erection of special Tribunaux has been brought about for children under thirteen and for those between thirteen and eighteen

The provisions compare very favourably if they do not considerably surpass those of our own Children Act, 1908

The main points are that children of either sex under thirteen years of age are not subject to punitive but rather to correctional jurisdiction They are not tried before a criminal Court, but the jurisdiction is civil in its nature, and the decisions of the Court are not inscribed " au casier judiciaire "

The Law of the 22nd July, 1912.

Article I—When found guilty they may be placed in charge of a guardian, in an educational establishment, in a charitable institute of recognised public utility, or in a public institution, as best meets the case

Article II.—Trials are held in private, the only persons admitted being " membres des comités de défense des enfants traduits en justice," such members of charitable institutions taking charge of children as may be admitted by the Court, and any person specially admitted

Article VI.—Special provision is also made for minors between thirteen and eighteen years of age who are guilty of infractions of the law Such persons cannot be directly cited before the ordinary criminal Courts, but may only be committed to such Courts by an examining magistrate (juge d'instruction). Art. XV.

Further provision for after supervision is made very like the supervision exercised on our own industrial and reformatory school boys who may be placed out on licence. Art. XX.

Interesting comparisons between the provisions of the Children Act and the New Law of France in these matters may well be made.

Children in Italy.

The following brief note on the legal position of the child in Italy will indicate that what has been said of Spain applies generally to the Latin countries

Although Italian scientists, philanthropists, and jurisconsults have for some time past devoted their attention to the problem of the social defence of the child against the evils that threaten his body and soul, yet unluckily very little has been done so far in Italy by the Government

The problem of the criminality of minors has attracted the notice of many sociologists, especially because this phenomenon has lately had a decided tendency towards increasing : in fact, the juvenile offenders sentenced in Italy in the year 1890 were 30,000, and now they are more than 50,000 per annum. Since 1906 the Press has taken an interest in the problem, and the provisions of the laws of the United States, and more especially those of the English Children Act, have been publicly discussed, and the Government has been invited to follow the example of other civilised nations. Unfortunately the financial difficulties always prevent good reforms from being carried into effect in Italy.

However, private initiative has tried to make up for the inaction of the State, and for some years there have been in all the important towns (Rome, Milan, Tunis, Florence, Genoa, Venice, Bologna, etc.) " Patronati perminorenni " (Societies for protection of juvenile offenders). These societies (which have lately received subsidies from the Government) are private : they are composed of young, willing and hard-working people who take upon themselves the unpleasant task of keeping a close watch on minors who have once committed a crime, and who have been acquitted or, having been sentenced, the Judge has ordered the sentence to be stayed during five years, and pardon to be granted if in this period they do not relapse into crime It is necessary that these children should be cared for, to prevent their becoming criminals, and therefore the members of the society go to inspect their houses, speak with their family, if any ; if not, arrangements are made for placing them in some school or reformatory or for sending them out to sea to become sailors, or suitable places may be found for them in shops or factories On Sundays and holidays they are assembled in a room, where good books are read, and good behaviour suitably rewarded. Many ladies have joined these societies, and carry on the noble work with the greatest devotion and self-sacrifice On representations received from these societies the Minister of Justice has ordered all juvenile offenders to be tried in a special audience, apart from other criminals

The Minister promised a special Act on the punishment and trial of offences committed by minors, and committees were appointed in both Houses of Parliament ; when and whether it will result in anything, we cannot say. Certainly the institution of special Children's Inspectors, probation officers, magistrates for juvenile offenders, etc., will entail no small expense, and the Italian budget seems already too much overburdened.

Meanwhile the new Code of Criminal Proceedings which took effect on the 1st January, 1914, has only one provision for the trial of minors (which see)

Still the private societies pursue their work of social redemption, and no doubt some good practical results have been achieved. These societies generally publish a yearly report of this work (these reports are not on sale).

A Congress of all Italian societies was held in Florence in the month of May, 1913, a report of which, by M. CASTELLANI, President of the Venetian Society and Judge of the Court of Appeal in Venice, is published in the *Rivisto di Diritto e Procedure Penale*, Milano. In relation to the Bill for a "Code for minors," see an Article by M. BERNAN, LL.D., in the same Review, Part 1, page 104. No particular book deals solely with the subject. The principal writers, however, are LINO FERRIANI, ALESSANDRO STOFFOTO (Professor of Criminal Law at the University of Bologna), G C. POLA, of Turin, and SCIPIO SIGHELE. See *Rivisto di Discipline Carcerarie*, and *La Scuola Positivo* (the Director of which is M ENRICO FENI, Professor of Criminal Anthropology at the University of Rome, M P. and a pupil of C. Lombrosso) See also the book by Professor FLORIAN, *I vagabondi*.

The following is an epitome of the Italian law concerning minors—

CRIMINAL CODE (OF THE YEAR 1890)

Section 21.—When a minor has been sentenced to one month's imprisonment, the judge may order him to expiate the sentence in his own house

Section 53 —He who, when he committed a crime, was still under nine years of age, shall not be proceeded against.

However, if the crime was punishable with penal servitude for life or with more than one year's imprisonment, the jury may order the minor to be placed in a reformatory for any period, but not beyond his coming of age (twenty-one years), or the judge can enjoin the parents or guardian to watch over the minor's conduct, under penalty of paying a fine not exceeding, 2,000 lire, if the minor relapses into crime.

Section 54 —He who, when he committed the crime, was more than nine but less than fourteen years old, is not liable to prosecution, unless his discernment be proved (compare English and French law).

Section 391.—Whoever maltreats a member of his family or a child under twelve years of age is punished with hard labour for not less than three days nor more than thirty months If the person maltreated be a son or a daughter, the penalty is from one to five years' hard labour.

Section 392.—In the cases contemplated by the foregoing paragraphs the judge may declare that, as an effect of his sentence, the parent shall not exercise any right arising from the parental authority (*patria potestas*) over the person and estate of the child, who has been injured by his crime.

Section 386 —Whoever abandons a child under twelve years of age . . . is liable to the punishment of hard labour from three to thirty months (English Children Act fixed sixteen as the age) If a serious injury to the body or mind results from the abandonment, the culprit is liable to a punishment of hard labour from thirty months to five years, and if death is caused, from five to twelve years

Section 387 —The penalty of the foregoing paragraph shall be increased by one-third—
  (a) if the child is abandoned in a lonely place ; or
  (b) if the crime is committed by the child's parents

Section 389 —Whoever, having found a child under seven years of age forsaken or lost . . . omits to inform the Authorities or their officials at once, is liable to a fine from 50 to 100 lire.

Section 390 —Whoever, abusing the means of correction or discipline, causes damage or danger to the health of a person under his authority, or entrusted to his care for the sake of education, treatment, or supervision, or for apprenticeship in a trade or profession, is liable to a punishment of from three days' to eighteen months' imprisonment.[1]

CODE OF CRIMINAL PROCEEDINGS (1913)

Section 373.—The trial shall always take place with closed doors whenever a minor under eighteen years stands accused

Section 372 —Any person apparently under eighteen years of age shall be prevented from entering a Criminal Court.

Section 423 —When a minor under eighteen years of age is sentenced for the first time to no more than one year's imprisonment, the judge may order the execution of the sentence to be stayed for the period of five years, subject to the offender's behaving well during that time—in which case he shall be pardoned (Compare English rules and Probation of Offenders)

AN ACT FORBIDDING THE EMPLOYMENT OF CHILDREN IN ITINERANT PROFESSIONS (1873)

(*Cf* France, December, 1874, as to "les professiones ambulantes ")

Section 1.—Whoever entrusts, for any cause whatever, to Italians or foreigners, persons of either sex under eighteen years of age, even if they are their own children or wards and whoever receives them with the purpose of employing them in any way in an itinerant profession, such as that of a mountebank, player, singer, rope-dancer, fortune-teller, wild beast showman, beggar, and the like, shall be punished with imprisonment for one to three months, and with a fine from 50 to 250 lires As a consequence of the sentence, the guardian shall lose his right to guardianship

Section 2 —Whoever has with himself, for the purpose of carrying

---
[1] Flogging as a means of correction has, of course, been abandoned in the schools

on one of the aforementioned professions, persons under eighteen years of age, who are not his own children, shall be punished with three to six months' imprisonment and a fine from 100 to 500 lire If the minor has been abandoned, or as a consequence of want of food, ill-treatment, or cruelty, has suffered a serious damage to his health, the imprisonment shall be from six to twelve months, unless the facts constitute a greater crime.

Section 3.—If the minor is taken abroad, the penalty of Section 1 shall be of six to twelve months' imprisonment and a fine of 100 to 500 lire (See English Law, 1913.)

Section 4—Italians who keep abroad a child under eighteen years for the purpose of employing him in one of the professions mentioned in this Act, are liable to a punishment of imprisonment from one to two years, and a fine from 500 to 1,000 lire If the minor has been forsaken and has suffered a bodily injury, the penalty may be increased to three years' imprisonment.

Section 5—Whoever carries away or causes to be carried away with violence or deceit, a minor under twenty-one years, or takes away with seduction a minor under eighteen years from his parents or guardians, in order to employ him in one of the professions mentioned in Section 1, is liable to a punishment of three to five years' hard labour.

AN ACT ON THE WORK OF WOMEN AND CHILDREN (1902)

Children under twelve years cannot be employed in any factory (Sec. 1) For work underground, as in mines, galleries, quarries, etc, boys under thirteen years and women of any age cannot be employed (Sec 1) For dangerous and unwholesome work, boys under fifteen and girls under age cannot be employed A medical certificate certifying the good health and fitness for work is necessary in order that a child may be admitted to work

Children must have a "service book" stating their name, age, profession, and when they have been vaccinated

Work by night is forbidden to boys under fifteen and girls under age (Sec. 5).

Children of either sex up to fifteen years cannot be employed for more than eleven hours out of the twenty-four (Sec 7).

Work of children cannot last for more than six hours uninterruptedly, but must be interrupted for a rest of one or two hours (Sec 8)

Offenders are liable to a fine from 50 to 5,000 lire, and the proceeds of these fines shall be added to the fund for old age and invalidity

In a Regulation attached to the Act, and in two Schedules, all the unwholesome and dangerous professions are enumerated, and other provisions are given as to the application of the Act

POLICE ACT (1889)

Section 113.—If the idler or vagabond is under eighteen years of age, the President of the Court, on the report of the Head Commissioner of the Police of the district, orders him to be consigned to his father or guardian, directing him to look after the education and watch over the conduct of the boy, under penalty of a fine up to 1,000 frcs. If the father or guardian persists in his neglect, he may be sentenced to lose the rights of parental authority or of guardianship

Section 114.—If the minor under eighteen years is without parents or guardians, or if they cannot look after his education, the President may order him to be placed with some honest family that consents to accept him, or in a reformatory, until he has learnt a trade, but not beyond his minority. The parents and relatives are bound to pay for the board, or for the part of it to be fixed by the Judge.

Section 115.—The provisions of the foregoing sections apply also to the case when the minor is an habitual beggar or prostitute.

Having briefly surveyed the attitude of the law in other countries, it is proposed to give a short bibliography with descriptions of more important works, and then to follow with a statement of English law relating to—

The protection, morally and physically, the education; and the restrictions on employment of children.

BIBLIOGRAPHY

Germany.

A VERY complete bibliography of this subject, as it applies to German speaking peoples, may be found in Miss Schultz's dissertation " Der strafrechtliche Schutz des Kindes, 1908." In addition may be mentioned the following, either not referred to by the above author, or published since 1908—

1 — *Klumker & Keller*, Säuglingsfürsorge und Kinderschutz in den europäischen Staaten, nennen, das 2 Bände umfasst und gebunden Mk 67 kostet

" The Care of Infants and the Protection of Children in European States," bound in two volumes (not to be had separately).

2 — *Agahd*, Gewerbl Kinderarbeit in Erziehungsanstalten — Reform, betr die Kinderarbeit in gewerbl. Betrieben . . 1905

" Child Labour in Homes and Reformatories—Reforms in Conditions of Child Labour in Factories " 1905

3 — *Agahd*, Kinderarbeit un Gesetz gegen die Ausnutzung kindl Arbeits kraft in Deutschland (unter Berücksichtigung der Gesetzgebung des Auslandes) . 1902

" Child Labour and the Law for the Prevention of sweated Labour for Children in Germany " (foreign law on the subject also considered) 1902

4 — *Agahd & v Schulz*, Gesetz betr die Kinderarbeit in gewerbl. Betrieben 3 Auflage 1905

" The Law concerning Child Labour in Industry," 3rd Edition 1905

5 — *Bittmann*, Die jugendlichen Arbeiter in Deutschland 1910

" The Youthful Workmen in Germany " . . 1910

6 — *Coelsch*, Deutsche Lehrlingspolitik im Handwerk . . 1910

" The System of Apprenticeship in Trade " . . 1910

7 — *Hell*, Jugendliche Schneiderinnen u Näherinnen in München 1911

" Young Taıloresses and Needlewomen in Munich " . . 1911

8 — *Kaup*, Jungendliche Arbeiter in Deutschland

" The Child Worker in Germany "

9 — *Jauch*, Gewerbl Lehrlingswesen in Deutschland (Mit besonderer Berücksichtigung Badens) 1911

" The System of Trade Apprenticeship in Germany with special reference to Baden " 1911

10 — *Jauch*, Lehrlingswesen und Berufserziehung des gewerbl. Nachwuchses 1912

" Apprenticeship and Training of the rising working generation " 1912

11 — *Rohmer*, Hausarbeitgesetz Erlautert . . 1912

" The Law of Home Employment " A discussion . . 1912

12 — *Hülsman*, Der Gegenstand des Rechtsschutzes mit bes Rücksicht des Strafrechts 1907

" The Protective Law with special reference to the Penal Code " 1907

13 — *Grüder*, Die strafrechtl Behandlung von Kindern u Jugendlichen im geltenden Recht u ein Vorentwurf zu einem deutschen Strafgesetzbuch . . . 1911

" The Legal Treatment of Children and Juvenile Workers according to the law in force, and an outline of the German Criminal Code "

14.—*Niczky*, Die Entwicklung des gesetzl Schutzes der gewerbl tatigen Kinder und jugendl Arbeiter in Deutschland (unter bes Berücksichtigung d Kinderschutzes v 30 Marz, 1903) . 1905

"The Development of Legal Protection of Children and Juvenile Workers employed in Germany" (The Law on the Protection of Children, of the 30th March, 1903, is specially discussed) 1905

Many of the above are pamphlets only. In addition the "International Association for the legal protection of workmen" (Internationalen Vereingung fur gesetzlichen Arbeiterschutz) has from time to time published pamphlets which touch on these matters

To indicate the importance of the child in the eyes of continental jurists and sociologists, attention may be drawn to a new magazine published quarterly under the title of *Fortschritte des Kinderschutzes und der Jugenfursorge* The editor is J Klumker, joint-author of the largest German work on the subject noted at the head of this bibliography Two numbers have been issued up to date, the first a treatise by SANDSBERG, entitled *Vormundschaftsgericht und Ersatzerziehung*, and the second, in December, 1913, a treatise by BENDER, *Der Schutz der gewerblich tatigen Kinder und der jugendlichen Arbeiter*

France.

Caire, César La législation sur le travail industriel des femmes et des enfants 1896
Debolo, Marcel docteur en droit L'Apprentissage a l'atelier 1906
Dolfus Franco, Eugène Essai historique sur la condition legale du mineur apprenti, ouvrier d'industrie ou employe de commerce . . 1900
Kleine L'enfant, ses amis, ses protecteurs, ses defenseurs
Note.—M Kleine has also written on the Juvenile Courts in Germany and in England—
  Les Tribunaux pour enfants en Allemagne 1910
  Les Tribunaux pour enfants en Angleterre 1908
Drucker, Gaston La protection des enfants maltraites et moralement abandonnes 1894
  A commentary on the law of the 24th July 1889
Leloir Etude sur la loi du 19 Avril, 1898, relative a la protection de l'Enfance
Passe Manuel de la defense des enfants traduits en justice 1910
André, Léonce La lutte contre la criminalite juvenile 1912
Vidal, Georges Cour de Droit Criminel et de Science penitentiaire 4 Ed . 1910

The juvenile criminal is fully considered in M Vidal's work, and in a manner unknown in English literature on this subject M Gardeil in the *Revue Pénitentiaire*, No 4, 1901, writing on the first edition of this work, says—

"L'étude de la minorité est particulièrement complète Partant de cette idée que l'augmentation de la criminalité juvénile est un fait social—non, comme le voudrait Lombroso manifestation d'une nécessité physiologique—s'appuyant sur les observations de MM Henri Joly, Raux, Ferriani, il démontre que les motifs de cette augmentation sont la désorganisation de la famille, le relâchement du lien familial, l'absence d'éducation, le défaut de surveillance des parents qui résulte souvent de l'organisation du travail industriel, le vagabondage, les mauvais conseils, les mauvais exemples des parents Il étudie ensuite la situation faite au mineur de seize ans par le Code pénal français et le mouvement d'idées qui se manifeste de plus en plus, tendant à substituer à la condamnation pénale l'internement de longue durée, considéré surtout comme un moyen d'éducation et de redressement , les modifications qui se sont produites depuis plusieurs années, dans la pratique judiciaire, à l'égard des mineurs, ont trouvé un appui dans les heureuses innovations des art 4 et 5 de la loi du 19 avril, 1898, malgré les lacunes[1] que présente encore cette loi Un tableau très intéressant des établissements pénitentiaires, soit publics, soit privés, ainsi qu'une statistique des résultats obtenus et des raisons qui ont influé sur ces résultats terminent cette étude très complète de la minorité"

Just as in Germany the study of child life from a legal point of view is deemed to be worth devoting a magazine to, so also in France a new Revue was established last year The first number of this *Revue des Tribunaux pour Enfants* was published on 15th December, 1913 It is under the joint-editorship of MM Paul Kahn and Jacques Teutsch, Avocats a la Cour d'Appel de Paris Its contributories include men whose names are famous in French legal circles—MM HENRI ROBERT, Bâtonnier de l'ordre des Avocats, DE VALLES, Président des Audiences de mineurs à la Cour de Paris, HONNORAT, Chef de la 1io division à la Prefecture de police, chef des services de la Protection de l'Enfance

The Revue consists of original articles, and of the text of new laws or projected laws dealing with the position of children in France and abroad It is to be published four times a year, between 15th November and 1st August

England.

English literature is very deficient in socio-legal matter Where the law is discussed, it is usually treated entirely as law, and not from the point of view of the sociologist, notwithstanding the fact

---

[1] The gaps above mentioned have been filled up by the new law already referred to as coming into force on the 4th of March, 1914 (see *Introduction*)

that the modern tendency of legislation is towards the protection of child life from the economic standpoint.

Encyclopaedia of Local Government Law. Vol. VI, Reformatory and Industrial Schools	1908
Simpson: Treatise on the Law and Practice relating to Infants 3rd Edition	1910
Hall & Pretty. The Children Act, 1908, being the 3rd Edition of "Hall's Law Relating to Children"	1909
Jones & Bellot. Law of Children and Young Persons (in relation to Penal Offences)	1909
Wyatt Education Acts, 1870-1902	1905
Owen Elementary Education Acts, 20th Edition	1903
Halsbury: Laws of England, Vol XII Education	1907
Renton Encyclopaedia of the Laws of England Vol XIII	1908
Bowstead Law Relating to Factories and Workshops	1901
Redgrave Factory and Workshop Acts 11th Edition	1909
Mews Digest of English Case Law down to 1907	1908
General Law Reports and Statutes	
National Society for the Prevention of Cruelty to Children, Reports from 1905-6	

TABLE OF CASES CITED

	PAGE
A and B (Infants), *In re* (1897), 1 Ch., D. 786	51
Agar-Ellis *v* Lascelles, *In re*, 10 Ch , Div 49	61
Barnardo *v* McHugh (1891), A C 388	50, 64
Barnes *v* Barnes, 1 P and D 463	55
Bell *v* Graham, 97 L T R 52	65
Belper School Attendance Com *v* Bailey, 9 Q B D 259	71
Bevan *v* Shears (1911), 2 K.B. 936 , 105 L T R 795	75
Ching *v* Surrey County Council (C A 1910), 1 K B 736 , 102 L T R , 414	46
Cleary *v* Booth (1893), 1 Q B 465 68 L T R. 349	20
Cole *v* Pendleton, 60 J P , 357	18
Director of Public Prosecutions *v* Witkowski, 104 L T R , 453	11
Field *v* Moore, 7 De G M and G , 691	58
Fitzgerald *v* Northcote, 4 F and F , 656	19
Guardians of Southwark *v* L C.C, 102 L T R , 747	16
Havelock *v* Havelock, 17 Ch D 807	58
Hewitt *v* Thompson, 53 J P , 103 , 60 L T 268	72
Holloway *v* Crow (1911), 1 K B 636 , 105 L T R 73	71
Hunter *v* Johnson, 12 Q B D 225	20
Isle of Wight County Council *v* Holland (1909), 101 L T R , 861	66, 72
Jones *v* Rowland, 80 L T R , 630	75
Lloyd *v* Grace, Smith & Co , 104 L T R , 789	49
London School Board *v* Bridge, *In re* Murphy (1872), 2 Q B D , 397	70
London School Board *v* Duggan, 13 Q B D , 176	71
London County Council *v* Hearn (1909), 78 L J , K B 414	68, 73
Macrae *v* Harness, 103 L T R , 629	59
Manders *v* Manders, 63 L T , 627	51
Mansell *v* Griffen, 98 L T R., 51, and 99 L T R , 133	19
Marshall *v* Graham, 97 L T R , 52	63, 65
Martin *v* Martin, 2 L T , 188	55
Mather *v* Lawrence (1899), 1 Q B , 1,000	123, 129
Meacher *v* Young, 2 My & K , 490	58
Mellor *v* Denham, 4 Q B D , 241	65, 119
Milton *v* Studd (1910), 2 K B , 118	8
Morris *v* Carnarvon County Council (C.A , 1910), 1 K B 840 , 102 L T R 524	46
Mozley Stark *v* Mozley Stark (now Hitchins) and Hitchins (1910), P 190	52
Murphy, *In re* (1872), 2 Q B D 397	70
Newton, *In re* (1896), 1 Ch 740	62
Plomley, *In re*, 45 L T R. 283	57

	PAGE
Powell *v* Powell (1900), 1 Ch 243	12
Pryor *v* Pryor (1900), P 157	55
Queen *v* Gyngall (1893), 2 Q B 232	54, 56
Reg *v.* Cox (1898), 1 Q B 179	16
—— *v* Falkingham, L R, 1 C C R, 222; 21 L T R 637	21
—— *v* Senior (1899), 1 Q B 283, 79 L T R 562	21
—— *v.* Shurmer, 17 Q B D 323, 55 L T R 126	34
—— *v* White, 24 L T, 637, L R, 1 C C R., 311	22
Rex *v.* Austin, *Ex parte* Leah, 96 L T 29, 71 J P 29	123
—— *v* Connor (1908), 2 K B 26, 98 L T R 932	17
—— *v* Dent, 71 J.P, 507	35
—— *v* Morris and others, W Riding Justices (1910), 2 K B 192	66, 69, 73
Robinson *v* Hill (1910), 1 K B 94, 101 L T R 573	127
Russon *v* Dutton (No 1), 104 L T R, 599	6
Saunders *v* Richardson, 7 Q B D 388	76
Scanlan, *In re*, 40 Ch., D 200	53, 62
Shelley *v* Westbrooke, 23 R R 47	57, 63
Shiers *v* Stevenson, 105 L T R 522	73
Shrimpton *v* Hereford County Council (H of L), 104 L T R 145	47
Smith *v* Martin, etc (C A 1911), 2 K B 775, 105 L T R 281	48
Stevenson *v* Goldstraw (1906), 2 K B 298, 95 L T R 111	119, 121
Strong *v* Treise (1909), 1 K B 613, 100 L T R 340	118
Thomassett *v* Thomassett (1894), P 295, 71 L T R 148	54
Wake *v* Dyer, 104 L T R 488	11
Walker *v* Cummings (1912) 107 L T R 304	75
Willis *v* Barron (1902), A C 271	12
Winyard *v* Toogood (1882), 10 Q B D 218	69
X *v* Y, *In re* (1899), 1 Ch 526	53

THE CHILD

ITS PROTECTION, EDUCATION, AND EMPLOYMENT

CHAPTER I

PROTECTION OF CHILDREN—THEIR MORAL WELFARE

MODERN legislation has taken into consideration the moral as well as the physical well-being of the child, and Lord Herschell's gibe that "the child was at length raised to the level of the dog" is no longer possible. The child's well-being has, during the last ten years, been most carefully considered, and no branch of legislation has made more rapid strides and shown greater daring in the direction of social reform than that in favour of children.

Provision is now made for the protection of the child, morally and bodily, not only against wanton neglect, but also in circumstances forming possible sources of danger to child-life, in which cases statutory provision is made for precautionary measures to be taken. Failure to take such precautions is, in some cases, a statutory offence, rendering those responsible for such failure to a liability to be proceeded against by indictment or in a Court of summary jurisdiction, e.g., overlaying of infants under three years of age by a person under the influence of drink is neglect amounting to cruelty and may amount to manslaughter.[1]

The protection afforded by various Acts relating to the employment of children will form the subject of a separate chapter, the two chapters following being restricted to the moral and physical welfare of the child.

Moral Welfare.

The Children Act, 1908,[2] makes special provision for the purely moral welfare of the child as well as for the moral welfare as likely

[1] 8 Ed. VII, Ch. 67, Secs. 12, 13
[2] 8 Ed. VII, Ch. 67

to influence the physical powers of the child and for the bodily welfare as distinct from the moral.

The provisions intended to protect the moral well-being and to guard against the creation of youthful criminals are chiefly contained in Part VI of the Act [1]

Clearing the Court during Examination of Children

In the trial of any case in relation to an offence against, or any conduct contrary to, decency or morality, the Court may direct that all or any persons not being members or officers of the Court or parties to the case their counsel or solicitors or persons directly concerned in the case, shall be excluded from the Court during the taking of the evidence of any person deemed by the Court to be a child or young person.[2] This provision is not to be a ground for excluding *bonâ fide* press representatives who are expressly excepted from the operation of the Act in this respect.

Exclusion of Children from Court.

Children, other than those actually implicated, may, in any trial of a person charged with any offence or in any proceedings preliminary to any trial, be ordered to be removed from the Court. A child implicated includes one charged with an offence or required as a witness in any case.[3] Since infants in arms cannot always be removed from the Court, such children are exempt from this provision as are clerks and messengers in attendance at a Court in connection with their employment

Purchase of Old Metals and Pawn.

One of the greatest incitements to dishonesty is the ease with which money can be raised by the sale of old materials such as old metals from buildings, which in youthful eyes are worthless

In order to remove or at any rate to mitigate this evil, old metal dealers[4] and marine store dealers[5] are prohibited from purchasing scrap or broken metal, partly manufactured metal goods, or old and defaced metal goods, from any person apparently under 16 years of age; whether such person be acting for himself or as agent for another The penalty imposed upon such dealers for

---

[1] 8 Ed VII, Ch 67, Secs 114 to 120   [2] Sec 114
[3] Sec 116   [4] 34 and 35 Vict, Ch 112
[5] 57 and 58 Vict., Ch. 60.

breach of this rule is a fine not exceeding £5, recoverable on summary conviction.[1]

Pawn.

Pawnbrokers in like manner are prohibited from taking in pawn any article from any person apparently under the age of fourteen years, whether such article be offered on his own behalf or on behalf of another Failure on behalf of a pawnbroker to observe this rule is punishable as an offence against the Pawnbrokers Act, 1872.[2]

Moral as Affecting Physical Well-being.

Having regard to the likelihood of injury to children by too early an indulgence in the habits of adults, the first decisive step towards the eradication of this evil as it relates to smoking is to be found in the Children Act, 1908 [3]

The provisions in this matter take the same form as most provisions in relation to children, that is, they aim at prevention at the source by providing against the sale of certain smoking materials to persons under the age of sixteen years

Selling Cigarettes Penalty.

If any person sells to a person apparently under the age of sixteen any cigarettes, cigarette papers, cut tobacco rolled up in paper, tobacco leaf, or other material in such form as to be capable of immediate use for smoking[4] whether for his own use or not, he shall be liable, on summary conviction, in the case of a first offence to a fine not exceeding £2, and in the case of a second offence to a fine not exceeding £5, and in the case of a third or subsequent offence to a fine not exceeding £10 [5]

Forfeiture of Tobacco.

Powers are given to constables and park-keepers in uniform to seize cigarettes or smoking materials as above described in the possession of any person apparently under the age of sixteen years, who is found smoking in any street or public place [6] Any such smoking materials so seized may be disposed of as the police authority directs when the seizure is made by the constable, or if

---

[1] 8 Ed VII, Ch 67, Sec 116
[2] 35 and 36 Vict, Ch 93
[3] 8 Ed VII, Ch 67, Secs 39 to 43
[4] Sec 43 (1)
[5] Sec 39
[6] Sec 40

the seizure is made by a park-keeper then at the direction of the authority by whom the keeper is appointed. The power to seize such materials extends to a power to search in the case of a boy but no keeper or constable is authorised to search a girl.[1]

The Act applies also to tobacco and substitutes for tobacco other than cigarettes and smoking materials as described in section 43 (1), but it is a good defence for a person selling such tobacco to show that he did not know, and had no reason to believe, that the young person purchasing was purchasing for his own use.[2]

There is nothing in the Act in relation to pipes, which therefore may not be seized, but any class of tobacco comes within the law and may be seized as described by a constable or park-keeper in uniform.

Automatic Machines.

The provisions of the law would be incomplete if it were possible for children and young persons to obtain cigarettes by other means than purchase from premises licensed for the sale of tobacco. All cases cannot be provided for, but provision is made against a too extensive use of automatic machines.[3]

Where such a machine is being extensively used by children and young persons a Court of summary jurisdiction may, on complaint, order the owner of such machine to take precautions to prevent the machine being used by children, or, if necessary, order the machine to be removed. Any persons aggrieved by the order of justices have the right to appeal to a Court of Quarter Sessions.[4] Failure to comply with an order in this respect is punished on summary conviction by a fine not exceeding £5, and a further fine not exceeding £1 for each day during the continuance of the offence.[5]

Exceptions.

The usual exceptions are made in favour of sales to messenger boys in uniform making purchases of smoking materials whilst employed as messengers. Young persons whilst in possession of such materials in the course of their employment by a manufacturer or dealer in tobacco, either wholesale or retail, may not be interfered with, and tobacco in their possession may not be seized.[6]

---

[1] Sec. 40   [2] Sec. 43, (2) and (3)   [3] Sec. 41
[4] Sec. 41   [5] Sec. 41 (2)   [6] Sec. 42

Sale of Intoxicants.

The first provisions as to intoxicants were not made in the Children Act, 1908, previous legislation having laid down certain regulations as to the serving of intoxicants to children and young persons. The more important protective enactments in this matter are now to be found in that Act [1] and in the Licensing (Consolidation) Act, 1910.[2]

In 1901[3] an Act was passed regulating the sale of intoxicants to children. This Act is now repealed by the Licensing (Consolidation) Act, 1910,[4] but substantially re-enacted by secs. 67 and 68, which provide as follows—

"67.—The holder of a justices' on-licence shall not sell or allow any person to sell, to be consumed on the premises, any description of spirits to any person apparently under the age of sixteen years."

The penalty for contravention of the section is a fine of 20s. for the first offence, and 40s. for any subsequent offence.

"68.—The holder of a justices' licence shall not knowingly sell or deliver or allow any person to sell or deliver, save at the residence or working place of the purchaser any description of intoxicating liquor to any person under the age of fourteen years for consumption on or off the premises excepting such intoxicating liquors as are sold or delivered in corked and sealed vessels in quantities not less than one reputed pint for consumption off the premises."

In relation to the sale of intoxicants there is a further offence which may be committed by persons not licence-holders. By section 68, sub-section 2, *any* person knowingly sending a child under fourteen to a place where intoxicants are sold, delivered, or distributed, for the purpose of obtaining any kind of intoxicating liquor, is guilty of an offence except in cases coming within the exception mentioned in sub-section 1.[5] For these offences of selling or sending for intoxicants the offender is liable to a fine of 40s. for the first offence and of £5 for any subsequent offence.

The Licensing (Consolidation) Act does not, however, by these provisions prevent a licensee from employing a member of his family, his servant, or apprentice as a messenger to deliver

---
[1] Secs. 119 and 120.
[2] 10 Ed. VII and 1 Geo. V, Ch. 24, Secs. 67 and 68.
[3] 1 Ed. VII, Ch. 27.   [4] 10 Ed. VII and 1 Geo. V, Ch. 24.
[5] In sealed bottles, etc. (*supra*).

intoxicating liquors, even although he is under the age limits laid down [1]

Exclusion from Bars.

The Children Act, 1908,[2] goes further than section 68 of the Licensing Act, 1910. It is provided in section 120 that the holder of a licence of any licensed premises shall not allow a child to be at any time in the bar of the licensed premises, except during the hours of closing. Any licensee offending against this provision and any person attempting to cause a contravention is liable to penalties similar to those imposed in section 68 of the Licensing Act, 1910.

The mere fact that a child is found in the bar of licensed premises constitutes an offence as against the licensee. If, however, he can show that he has used due diligence to prevent the child being admitted to the bar, or that it was apparently over fourteen, he can rebut the charge.

This is a most far-reaching provision, and in order that it may not be unduly severe and oppressive, exceptions are made in the case of children of the licensee, and children residing on, but not employed on, the premises. Further, merely passing through a bar to another part of the premises, not being a bar, where there is no other convenient way to pass, is quite lawful and the Act does not, under the term "bar," include railway refreshment rooms or other premises intended in good faith for any purpose to which the holding of a licence is merely auxiliary.

Definition of "A Bar."

A bar of licensed premises means any open drinking bar, or any part of the premises exclusively or mainly used for the sale and consumption of intoxicating liquor. Thus a public coffee room in an hotel would not come under the head of a bar.

In *Russon (app) v Dutton (resp) (No 1)*[3] the appellant held a licence for an inn and his wife carried on a dressmaking business on an upper floor. Two girls, one aged ten, entered the premises for the purpose of obtaining a coat and skirt from the dressmaker. The appellant's wife invited them into the bar parlour to wait while she fetched the skirt. The girls were in the bar parlour for

---

[1] Sec 68, ss. 3 [2] 8 Ed VII, Ch 67, sec 120
[3] 104 L T R , 599.

a few minutes but the appellant had not seen them enter and could not know that they were there. He was, however, summoned and convicted. Lord Alverstone, C.J., in giving judgment refused to express an opinion as to whether a bar parlour is or is not a bar within the meaning of the Children Act, 1908. He, however, held that under the circumstances the appellant was not responsible for the action of his wife, who was not shown to have taken part in the management of the house, and as the justices had not found that there was any want of due diligence on the appellant's part, the conviction was quashed.

Giving Intoxicants.

It is now an offence punishable by a fine not exceeding £3 if any person gives intoxicating liquor to a child under the age of five years except on medical advice or in case of sickness or other necessity. The advice must be that of a duly qualified medical man or urgent cause must be shown.[1]

Begging.

Begging and street trading are two phases of lower class life which have a tendency to lead children into a life of vagabondage and vagrancy. The former is provided against in the Children Act, 1908,[2] the latter in the Employment of Children Act, 1903.[3]

Section 14 of the Children Act, 1908, provides—

"If any person causes or procures any child or young person, or having the custody, charge, or care[4] of a child or young person, allows that child or young person to be in any street, premises or place for the purpose of begging or receiving alms or of inducing the giving of alms, whether or not there is any pretence of singing, playing, performing, offering anything for sale, or otherwise, that person shall, on summary conviction, be liable to a fine not exceeding twenty-five pounds or alternatively or in default of payment of such fine, or in addition thereto, to imprisonment, with or without hard labour, for any term not exceeding three months."

Presumption as to Liability.

Further, if a person having the custody, charge, or care of a child or young person is charged with an offence under this section, and

---

[1] Children Act, 1908, Sec. 119. [2] Sec. 14.
[3] See *infra*. [4] See "Cruelty" for definition, p. 16.

it is proved that the child or young person was in any street, premises or place for such purpose, and that the person charged allowed the child or young person to be in the street, premises or place, he is presumed to have allowed him to be there for that purpose until the contrary be proved.

Betting with Infants.

Betting is one of the evils against which the legislature has endeavoured to protect infants. A wider view of infancy is taken in relation to betting than in the case of smoking and matters relating to intoxicants. The infancy coming within the Betting and Loans (Infants) Act, 1892,[1] endures until the age of twenty-one years is reached.

Betting and Loans Act, 1892.

It is provided by section 1 of this Act that if anyone, for the purpose of earning commission, reward or other profit, sends, or causes to be sent, to a person whom he knows to be an infant any circular . . or other document which invites or may reasonably be implied to invite the person receiving it to make any bet or wager, or to apply to any person or at any place with a view to obtaining information or advice for the purpose of any bet or wager, or for information as to any race upon which betting or wagering is generally carried on, such person so sending shall be guilty of a misdemeanour, and if convicted shall be liable to penalties.

Presumption of Infancy.

By section 3 it is further provided that if such a circular as above mentioned is sent to any person at any University, college, school or other place of education and such person is in fact an infant, it will be presumed that the sender or person causing the document to be sent knew the recipient to be an infant. This presumption is rebutted by the proof that the sender had reasonable ground to believe the recipient to be of full age

In *Milton* (app.) v. *Studd* (resp.)[2] the question as to what being "at any University" meant was raised. A letter inviting E. F S to apply to the appellant for information about a horse-race was

---
[1] 55 and 56 Vict, Ch. 4.
[2] (1910) 2 K B, 118, 102 L.T.R, 573.

sent on the instructions of M, the appellant, to an address in Cambridge which was not the University but a lodging house licensed by the University for the residence of undergraduates at the University. E. F. S was in fact an infant at the University It was held, Lord Alverstone dissenting, that where a person sends a betting circular to an infant undergraduate at an address in a University town, such an address being in fact a lodging house licensed by the authorities of the University, but the sender of the circular is unaware that the receiver is an infant or an undergraduate and that the address is a licensed lodging, the sender cannot be deemed to have known that the receiver is a "person at any University" within section 3 of the Betting and Loans (Infants) Act, 1892 [1]

In his judgment Mr Justice Bray said—

"I am sorry to have to come to this conclusion, as our decision may prove a source of mischief The section[2] imputes knowledge that the receiver is an infant under certain circumstances It imputes that knowledge only from a fact which shows knowledge from another thing Section 3 must be construed as referring to sending to a person at a University by some description which shows that the person knew he was sending to a University When it is sent to a wholly ambiguous address, it is impossible to infer knowledge from that"

Betting in the Streets with Infants.

By the Street Betting Act, 1906,[3] provision is made whereby an offence of frequenting or loitering in the streets or in public places for the purpose of book-making, betting or wagering, or of paying, receiving or settling bets is rendered more serious if any transaction is proved to have taken place with a person under sixteen years of age

"(1) Any person frequenting or loitering in streets or public places, on behalf either of himself or of any other person for the purpose of book-making, or betting, or wagering, or agreeing to bet or wager, or paying or receiving or settling bets, shall . .

(c) in the case of a third or subsequent offence, or in any case where it is proved that the person whilst committing the offence had any betting transaction with a person under the age of sixteen years, be liable on conviction on indictment to a fine not exceeding fifty pounds or to imprisonment, with or without hard

---

[1] 55 and 56 Vict, Ch. 4. [2] Sec. 3 [3] 6 Ed. VII, Ch. 43

labour, for a term not exceeding six months without the option of a fine, or on conviction under the Summary Jurisdiction Acts to a fine not exceeding thirty pounds or to imprisonment, with or without hard labour, for a term not exceeding three months, without the option of a fine."

First and second offences not aggravated by betting with young persons are punishable on summary conviction by fines not exceeding ten and twenty pounds respectively.

Presumption of Age.

As under most other protective Acts in favour of children, the age may be presumed, the Act[1] providing that any person who appears to the Court to be under sixteen years of age shall for the purpose of the Act be deemed to be under that age unless the contrary be proved, or unless the person charged shall satisfy the Court that he had reasonable grounds for believing otherwise.

Similar provisions to those contained in section 1 of the Betting and Loans (Infants) Act, 1892, in relation to betting are made in respect of soliciting infants to borrow money.

Loans to Infants.

Loans to infants are void under the Infants Relief Act, 1874,[2] but the following further provision is made by the Betting and Loans Act[3]—

"If anyone for the purpose of earning interest, commission, reward, or other profit, sends or causes to be sent to a person whom he knows to be an infant any circular, notice, advertisement, letter, telegram, or other document which invites or may reasonably be implied to invite the person receiving it to borrow money, or to enter into any transaction involving the borrowing of money, or to apply to any person or at any place with a view to obtaining information or advice as to borrowing money, he shall be guilty of a misdemeanour."

If any such document as above-mentioned sent to an infant purports to issue from any address named therein, or indicates any address as a place at which application is to be made with reference to the subject matter of the document, and at that place there is any business carried on in connection with loans, whether making or procuring loans or otherwise, every person who attends at such place for the purpose of taking part in, or who takes part in,

---

[1] 6 Ed. VII, Ch. 43, Sec. 1 (3)   [2] 37 and 38 Vict., Ch. 62, Sec. 1
[3] 55 and 56 Vict., Ch. 4, Sec. 2

or assists in the carrying on of such business shall be deemed to have sent such document or caused it to be sent, unless he proves that he was not in any way a party to and was wholly ignorant of the sending of such document

Amendment as to Presumption of Age.

There is no corresponding section relating to loans similar to section 3 in relation to betting circulars, but the Moneylenders Act, 1900,[1] has made the following provision—

" Where, in any proceedings under section 22 of the Betting and Loans (Infants) Act, 1892, it is proved that the person to whom the document was sent was an infant, the person charged shall be deemed to have known that the person to whom the document was sent was an infant, unless he proved that he had reasonable ground for believing the infant to be of full age "

Liability Under the Act.

The liability of a person on whose account circulars were sent was discussed in *Director of Public Prosecutions (app) v Witkowski (resp)*[2] In this case information was laid against the respondent who carried on business as a moneylender He gave instructions to his clerk to send moneylending circulars to captains and lieutenants in the army He knew that many second-lieutenants were minors, and he told his clerk to send to captains and lieutenants but not to second-lieutenants Without his knowledge the clerk sent a circular to a second-lieutenant who was in fact under age The circular invited the recipient to borrow money The magistrate held that the respondent did not send or cause to be sent the circular to the minor, but that, if he was bound by the act of his clerk, he had reasonable ground for believing all persons to whom the circulars were sent were of full age and he dismissed the summons It was held, dismissing the appeal, that the facts justified the finding

Lord Alverstone's judgment in the case[3] is interesting and important and so worthy of note—

" Respondeat Superior " in Criminal Cases.

" This case raises an important point As we had to point out a short time ago in the case of *Wake* v *Dyer*[4] with regard to the

---

[1] 63 and 64 Vict , Ch 51, Sec 5
[2] 104 L T R 453
[3] 104 L T R 455
[4] 104 L T R , 448

maxim *Respondeat Superior* in criminal cases much depends upon the true view of the statute creating the offence. . . . There is one class of cases under the Food and Drugs Acts, the Merchandise Marks Acts, and the Licensing Acts in which the Courts have decided that, where the Act is prohibited, the master is responsible for the criminal act of his servant, though he knew nothing about it. In the other class of cases relating to nuisances and to breaches of statutes in regard to obstructions on railways and the like, it has been held that the master is not responsible unless he had knowledge of, or was party to, the act complained of I doubt whether it can be said that the Betting and Loans (Infants) Act, 1892, is sufficiently strong to oblige us to say that any sending of these circulars to infants was intended to be absolutely prohibited."

Hence it would seem that the maximum *Respondeat Superior* does not apply in this case if the principal can prove that he had reasonable ground for believing the person receiving the circular to be of full age although his agent actually sent to a person who was an infant.

Undue Influence.

Apart from any statutory enactment, equity always interfered to relieve a child who had made an improvident bargain under presumed undue influence The age during which relief was and is still given is not necessarily infancy, but infancy will make the interference all the more likely.

The presumption arises chiefly in connection with gifts, but sales may equally be set aside The presumption does not arise until relationship between the parties is proved to be such as is likely to give one an influence over the other, e g , father to child, guardian to ward This presumption is not conclusive by reason of relationship [1]

Until it is shown that a child has outgrown parental influence the Court will presume that a gift by a child to its parent is made under the parent's influence unless it is evident that the child acted on independent advice. [2]

Children (Employment Abroad) Act, 1913.

Several Acts of Parliament deal with restrictions on the employment of children, but these are in the main directed towards the

---

[1] *Willis* v *Barron* (1902), A C 271
[2] *Powell* v *Powell* (1900), 1 Ch 243.

physical welfare of the child A new attitude is taken up in the Children (Employment Abroad) Act, 1913,[1] an Act to prohibit and restrict children and young persons being taken out of the United Kingdom with a view to singing, playing, performing, or being exhibited for profit. Its object is to prevent children and young persons engaged for places of entertainment abroad—quite genuinely in the first instance—drifting away into low class and dangerous engagements later

No person is allowed to take any child or young person out of the Kingdom for the above-mentioned purpose without a licence from a Metropolitan Police Magistrate [2] Under the new Act it is necessary to obtain the licence of a magistrate at Bow Street[3] before any child can be taken out of the United Kingdom for the purpose of singing, playing, performing, or being exhibited for profit This can only be obtained if the application is made with the consent of the parent or guardian of the young person, if the child is going to a particular engagement and is fit to undertake it, and proper provision has been made for the health, kind treatment, and adequate protection of the young person while abroad Arrangements have also to be made to ensure the return of the child-artist to the United Kingdom at the expiration of the engagement or on the revocation of the licence, and a copy of the agreement of employment in a language understood by the young person must be in the young person's possession [4]

In Charge of the Consul.

Section 2 of the Act provides that a licence shall not be granted for more than three months, but may be renewed by the police magistrate from time to time for a like period on a satisfactory report from the consular agent or other trustworthy person that the conditions of the licence are being complied with The magistrate may require recognisances or securities for the observance of the conditions of the licence, and for the future the child performer abroad will be practically the ward of the British Consul, who will be informed through the Secretary of State of the particulars of the licence The penalties for an offence against the Act are a fine not exceeding £100 or three months imprisonment, or both If by

---

[1] 3 and 4 Geo V, Ch 7   [2] Sec 1   [3] Secs 2 and 4
[4] Sec 2 (See *Introduction* as to Law of Italy on this point)

false pretences a child is persuaded to go abroad contrary to the Act the liability is imprisonment on indictment for a term not exceeding two years, with or without hard labour

Having thus examined the provisions of the law relating to the protection of child life from a moral point of view, we will next proceed to deal with the question of protection from physical violence and from injury affecting bodily, mental, and moral health

CHAPTER II

PROTECTION OF CHILDREN—THEIR PHYSICAL WELFARE. CRUELTY TO CHILDREN AND YOUNG PERSONS

ALTHOUGH the moral welfare of the child has but recently received the attention of the legislature, the physical well-being has for many years received a certain amount of attention. It is now twenty years since the Prevention of Cruelty to Children Act, 1894, was passed, and many amendments have been made during the last ten years.

The Prevention of Cruelty to Children Act, 1904,[1] repealed the provisions of the Prevention of Cruelty to Children Act, 1894,[2] and the former enactment has in its turn been partly repealed, but in substance re-enacted and amended by the Children Act, 1908.[3]

The main provision as to cruelty is now contained in the Children Act and is to the following effect—

Offences of Cruelty.

" If any person over the age of sixteen years, who has the custody, charge, or care of any child or young person, wilfully assaults, ill-treats, neglects, abandons, or exposes such child or young person, or causes or procures such child or young person to be assaulted, ill-treated, neglected, abandoned, or exposed, in a manner likely to cause such child or young person unnecessary suffering or injury to his health (including injury to or loss of sight, or hearing, or limb, or organ of the body, and any mental derangement) that person shall be guilty of a misdemeanour."[4]

Child and Young Person.

The material amendment in the Children Act in relation to the offence of cruelty seems to be the division of children under sixteen into two classes. A " child " is defined as a person under fourteen, whilst the expression " young person " means a person who is fourteen years of age or upwards and under the age of sixteen years.[5] The Prevention of Cruelty to Children Act, 1904, still

---

[1] 4 Ed VII, Ch 15   [2] 57 and 58 Vict, Ch 41
[3] 8 Ed VII, Ch 67   [4] 8 Ed VII, Ch 67, Sec 12
[5] 8 Ed VII, Ch 67, Sec 131.

applies as to the presumption of the age of the child [1] and it would perhaps follow that the age of a young person could be similarly presumed

Presumption of Age.

If, in the opinion of the Court, a child appears to be under a certain age, he shall be deemed to be under that age unless the contrary is proved. If an attempt is made by the defence to rebut the presumption, it will be necessary to produce evidence of age Any kind of material evidence will suffice, it being unnecessary to produce the actual birth certificate of the child [2]

The onus of proof where the defendant's age is in dispute is on the prosecution, but an indictment on such charges of a person whose age is so near sixteen as to raise a doubt would be unusual.

It should be noted that the statutes relating to children are preventive in character, and it is unnecessary to prove that a child or young person has actually suffered The likelihood of unnecessary suffering or injury to health must be demonstrated

Custody, Charge, or Care.

The person liable to be charged with cruelty is the person over sixteen having the *custody, charge, or care* of the child or young person. This, *primâ facie*, means the parent, but the term "parent" must be interpreted to include the step-parent of the child or young person, and any person cohabiting with the parent of the child [3] whether in lawful wedlock or not "Parent" also includes guardian and every person who is by law liable to maintain a child [3] This interpretation is placed upon the expression "parent" in the majority of cases in which the maintenance or employment of the children is in question On another point it has been decided [4] that the Board of Guardians are not included in the expression "persons liable to maintain"

It has been provided by the Prevention of Cruelty to Children Act, 1904, [5] that for the purpose of that Act

(*a*) Any person who is a parent of a child shall be presumed *to have the custody* of the child, and

---

[1] 4 Ed VII, Ch 15, Sec 17
[2] *R v Cox* (1898), 1 Q B 179
[3] 4 Ed VII, Ch 15, Sec 23
[4] *Guardians of Southwark v London County Council*, 102 L T R 747
[5] 4 Ed VII, Ch 15, Sec 23 (3)

(*b*) Any person to whose charge a child is committed by its parent shall be presumed to have *charge* of the child, and

(*c*) Any other person having actual possession or control of a child shall be presumed to have *the care* of a child.

The Children Act, 1908,[1] more fully provides that—

(*a*) Any person who is the parent or legal guardian of a child or young person or is legally liable to maintain a child or young person shall be presumed to have *the custody* of the child or young person, and as between father and mother, the father shall not be deemed to have ceased to have the custody of the child or young person by reason only that he has deserted, or otherwise does not reside with the mother and child or young person,[2] and

(*b*) Any person to whose charge a child or young person is committed by any person who has the custody of the child or young person shall be presumed to have *charge* of the child or young person, and

(*c*) Any other person having actual possession or control of a child or young person shall be presumed to have *the care* of the child or young person

Hence it may be seen that a father who has deserted his wife, being still deemed to have the custody of his child, will be liable for the offence of wilfully neglecting his child if he fails to provide adequate food, clothing, medical aid or lodging [3]

Custody.

The question of the custody of a child was discussed in *Rex* v. *Connor*.[4] Connor having deserted his wife and children, leaving them without money or food, was charged with unlawfully and wilfully neglecting his children in a manner likely to cause unnecessary suffering and injury to their health It was proved that the children, notwithstanding the assistance of friends and neighbours, were without sufficient food, and that Connor had provided neither food nor money to provide food, though he was earning wages and knew of their condition The jury found Connor guilty. The questions reserved for the Court were—

(1) Was Connor a person having the custody of his children

---

[1] 8 Ed VII, Ch 67, Sec 38 (2)
[2] *R* v *Connor*, 98 L T R 932, and (1908) 2 K B 26
[3] 8 Ed VII, Ch 67, Sec 12
[4] Crown cases reserved 124 L T Jour 526, and (1908) 2 K B 26

within the meaning of the Prevention of Cruelty to Children Act, 1904, he being absent from them ?[1] and

(2) Was Connor's omission wilful neglect within the meaning of the Act?

The Court held that Connor being the parent of the children was the person having the custody[2] of the children, and the fact that he had deserted them would not rebut the presumption, and further the failure to supply money for the children's support constituted neglect[3] within the meaning of the statute[4]. The decision in *Cole* v. *Pendleton* was approved by the Court as being a decision binding on the Court although the Poor Law Amendment Act, 1868,[5] is not now in force.

The case of *Rex* v *Connor* seems to be the basis of the extended definitions of "custody" and "neglect" in the Children Act[6] The provision is of considerable importance as it would be against public policy if the wilful abandonment of parental duty was sufficient to detach a father from his obligations as such

The only difficulty which now exists is that where the children are sufficiently maintained by their relatives or friends other than parents, the parent may still avoid his obligations. It is only where there is starvation, neglect, or a likelihood that suffering will ensue that the parent comes within the law, unless the second sub-section of section 12 applies, viz —

"A person may be convicted of an offence under section 12, either on indictment or by a Court of summary jurisdiction, notwithstanding that actual suffering or injury to health or the likelihood of such suffering or injury to health, was *obviated* by the action of another person."

Wilful Cruelty.

In order that an offence may be committed under this Act it must be wilful, that is, deliberate and with intention Every deliberate act is not necessarily wilful, as it is especially provided in the Children Act, 1908,[7] that the Act, like the Prevention of Cruelty to Children Act, 1904,[8] is not to be so construed as to

---

[1] Now settled by the Children Act, 1908, Sec. 12
[2] 4 Ed VII, Ch 15, Sec 23 (3) repealed, but re-enacted in Children Act, 1908
[3] *Cole* v *Pendleton*, 60 J P 357
[4] Children Act, Sec 38 (2)
[5] Sec 37
[6] Sec 12 and Sec 38 (2)
[7] 8 Ed VII, Ch 67, Sec 37
[8] 4 Ed VII, Ch 15

take away or affect the right of any parent, teacher, or other person having the lawful control or charge of a child or young person to administer punishment to such child or young person

Right to Punish.

The right of a parent to punish his child moderately and with propriety is a common law right which the Courts have always sustained. The teacher's right to punish is vested in him by an express or implied delegation.[1] If nothing is said in this relation when the child is placed in school the common law implies that the parent has delegated his right to the teacher. It is quite impossible for either an education authority or a principal teacher to delegate the right. An education authority has no right to punish and can neither delegate such right nor deny it,[2] while a principal teacher's right is itself delegated and the maxim *delegatus non potest delegare* applies. An assistant teacher fully qualified and in charge of a class has this delegated right direct from the parent in a proper case to punish, and where punishment is *properly* administered by him no assault or cruelty is committed, despite the regulations of a local authority to the contrary.[3] The offence committed is a breach of the terms of employment which are that he shall refrain from exercising his common law right to punish, delegated to him by the parent.

Blackstone.

On the right to punish, Blackstone[4] says—

"The power of a parent by our English laws . . . is sufficient to keep the child in order and obedience. He may lawfully correct his child, being under age, in a reasonable manner; for this is for the benefit of his education . . . He may also delegate part of his parental authority, during his life, to the *tutor or schoolmaster* of his child; who is then *in loco parentis*, and has such a portion of the power of the parent committed to his charge, viz., that of restraint and correction, as may be necessary to answer the purpose for which he is employed."

Mansell v. Griffin.

The expression "tutor or schoolmaster" may be interpreted

---

[1] *Fitzgerald v. Northcote*, 4 F. & F. 656
[2] *Mansell v. Griffin*, 98 L.J.K. 51
[3] *Mansell v. Griffin supra*   [4] Commentaries, Vol. 1, pp. 452, 453

very broadly without introducing any idea of sub-delegation, which theory is perhaps not altogether without legal authority [1] The question is, however, fully decided in the words of Mr Justice Phillimore in *Mansell* v *Griffin* [2]

" The authority of the head teacher in a public elementary school to inflict punishment extends to a responsible assistant teacher who is in charge of the education and discipline of a class "

On an appeal, this point was not in question and Lord Alverstone, C.J., refused to express an opinion [3] The decision of the Court in *Mansell* v *Griffin* would doubtless have been different had the parent of the child been aware that the local education authority forbade its assistants to administer punishment, and the parent sent the child to school relying on his knowledge and faith in the regulations As to whipping under the Children Act, see *Rex.* v. *Lydford.* [4]

Assaults, Ill-treats, Neglects.

The term "assault" has a very wide meaning indeed ; it is not necessary that any act of physical violence shall be perpetrated ; the mere offer to do bodily hurt with a present intention and ability is sufficient If such attempts or offers of physical violence are likely to effect either bodily or mental injury the offence is complete

Although a parent or teacher has the right to punish, this right must be exercised in a judicious manner. To detain a child after school hours may amount to an assault.[5] To lock a child in a room under circumstances tending to injure its health by fear causing mental suffering would, if done wilfully, amount to an act of cruelty comprised in the term "assault" The reasonableness of the punishment in such a case is a matter of fact depending on such circumstances as age, sex, and general health of the child.

The combination of words, "assaults, ill-treats, neglects, abandons, or exposes," is an attempt to include all forms of cruelty likely to cause injury The expression "*ill-treats*" would cover all forms of cruelty tending to injure, but it may be suggested that ill-treatment is systematic

---

[1] *Cleary* v *Booth* (1893), 1 Q B 465 & 68 L T R 349
[2] 98 L T R 51   [3] 99 L T R 133   [4] (Ct of Ap , 1914), 136 L T J 452
[5] *Hunter* v *Johnson*, 12 Q B D 225

Neglects.

The Children Act [1] provides that a parent or other person legally liable to maintain the child or young person shall be deemed to have neglected him in a manner likely to cause injury to his health if he fails to provide adequate food, clothing, medical aid, or lodging for the child or young person, or if being unable otherwise to provide such food, clothing, medical aid, or lodging he fails to take steps to procure the same to be provided under the Acts relating to the relief of the poor

The provision that failure to provide medical aid amounts to neglect is a statutory confirmation of judicial decisions, it having been laid down by Lord Russell, L C J , [2] that " at the present day when medical aid is within reach of the humblest and poorest members of the community, it cannot reasonably be suggested that the omission to provide medical aid for a dying child does not amount to neglect "

Abandonment and Exposure.

Abandonment and exposure are offences that have caused the bulk of litigation, but it is well settled what the limits are It is not necessary to prove actual suffering, the risk of suffering or likelihood of injury being sufficient [3]

R. v. Falkingham.

In *R. v. Falkingham*, the mother of a child packed it in a hamper with shavings and cotton-wool and forwarded it by train to the father's home. It was labelled "*With care, to be delivered immediately,*" and was in fact delivered in little over an hour Three weeks later the child died in the workhouse from other causes, but on the question being raised in the Court for Crown Cases Reserved it was held that the prisoner was properly convicted of abandonment.

R. v. White.

This case was tried under the provisions of the Offences against the Person Act, 1861, [4] and there could be little doubt about its

---

[1] 8 Ed VII, Ch 67, Sec 12 (1)
[2] In *R v Senior* (1899), 1 Q B 283, 79 L.T R. 562
[3] *R v Falkingham*, L R 1, C C R 222, and 21 L T R 637
[4] 24 and 25 Vict , Ch 100, Sec 27

application to the provisions of the Children Act. The case of *R. v. White*[1] was under the same Act.[2] In this case where a husband living apart from his wife allowed his child under two years of age to remain lying on the door-step where it had been placed by his wife to his knowledge, until it was cold and stiff, it was held that he had abandoned it.

In order to cause parents of young children to exercise care, the "over-laying" of a child under three years of age by a person under the influence of drink amounts to neglect likely to cause injury to health. As this question cannot arise unless death ensues, the provision is framed as follows[3]—

Suffocation of Child under Three.

"Where it is proved that the death of an infant under three years of age was caused by suffocation (not being suffocation caused by disease or the presence of any foreign body in the throat or air passages of the infant) whilst the infant was in bed with some other person over sixteen years of age, and that other person was, at the time of going to bed, under the influence of drink, that other person shall be deemed to have neglected the infant in a manner likely to cause injury to its health" within the meaning of section 12 of the Children Act, 1908.

Like the offences of cruelty set out in section 12 this offence is punishable either summarily or on indictment. Unless the charge is merely one of assault, a prisoner has the right to a trial by jury since the punishment which can be meted out is more than three months' imprisonment.[4]

Punishment on Indictment.

On indictment, the maximum punishment is a fine of £100, or alternatively, or in default, or in addition, imprisonment with or without hard labour for two years. If it is shown that the person convicted was directly or indirectly interested in any sum of money accruable or payable in event of the death of the child or young person on whom the cruelty was inflicted, the fine may be increased to £200, or instead of any other penalty penal servitude for any

---

[1] 24 L T 637, L R 1, C C R 311
[2] Offences against the Person Act, 1861
[3] Children Act, 1908, Sec 13
[4] 42 and 43 Vict, Ch 49, Sec 17 (Summary Jurisdiction Act, 1879)

term not exceeding five years may be inflicted[1] provided that the person convicted knows that such sum is payable

On Summary Conviction.

On summary conviction a fine not exceeding £25 may be inflicted or alternatively, or in default, or in addition, imprisonment for any term not exceeding six months with or without hard labour.[2] In awarding sentence in a Court of summary jurisdiction the fact that the prisoner was interested in any money payable on the child's death must be taken into account[3] Such person is deemed to have an interest if any share or benefit accrues to him although the money is not legally payable to him.

Magistrates may, where of the opinion that the punishment they may inflict is inadequate, commit the person charged for trial.

Manslaughter.

Where, as may well be, in case of the victim's death from cruelty a charge of manslaughter is preferred, the jury may find the person charged guilty of the offence of cruelty under section 12 It may be noted, however, that the death of the child or young person in respect of whom the offence is committed does not take away the right to proceed either by indictment or in a summary way under the Act.[4]

Evidence.

A copy of a policy of insurance, certified by an officer or agent of the company granting the policy, to be a true copy, shall in any proceedings on an offence of cruelty be *primâ facie* evidence that the child or young person therein stated to be insured has been in fact so insured, and that the person in whose favour the policy has been granted is the person to whom the money thereby assured is legally payable

Risk of Burning.

Besides the offences of cruelty enumerated in section 12 of the Children Act, 1908, provision is made to guard against parental negligence[5] by requiring that any open fire-grate in a room in which

---

[1] Children Act, 1908, Sec 8 (5) [2] Sec 12 (1)
[3] Sec 12 (5)   [4] Sec. 12 (3)   [5] Sec 15

a child *under* seven is allowed must be sufficiently protected to guard the child against the risk of being burnt or scalded. If by reason of failure on the part of any person over sixteen to guard such a child in his custody, the child is killed or suffers serious injury, he is liable on summary conviction to a fine not exceeding £10, and may also, when the negligence is sufficient to warrant it, be indicted for manslaughter.

Flannelette Danger.

A further Act, called the Misdescription of Fabrics Act,[1] aims at the physical safety of children, and provides that it shall not be lawful for any person to "sell, or expose, or have in his possession for sale, any textile fabric, either in the piece or made up into garments, or in any other form, to which is attributed expressly or inferentially the quality of non-inflammable, or safety from fire: unless such fabric conforms to such standard of non-inflammability as may be prescribed by regulation to be made by the Secretary of State." The penalty will be a fine not exceeding £10 for the first offence, and in second or subsequent offences £50.

This Act is designed to deal with the "flannelette danger," and its enforcement is delegated to the local authorities, who will appoint male or female inspectors with power, if authorised by the local authority, to institute and carry on proceedings.

Summary Powers.

Where any of the offences enumerated in the Children Act, namely cruelty,[2] permitting a child to beg,[3] exposing it to danger of suffocation,[4] or risk of burning,[5] allowing a child or young person to frequent a brothel,[6] or allowing a young girl to be prostituted[7] is committed, powers are granted for the greater safety of and speedier justice to the child or young person.[8] The same powers are granted when any offence under sections 27, 55, or 56 of the Offences against the Person Act, 1861,[9] or any offence against a child or young person under sections 5, 42, 43, 52, or 62 of that Act, or under the

---

[1] Fabrics (Misdescription) Act, 1913, 3 and 4 Geo V, Ch 17
[2] Sec 12
[3] Sec 14
[4] Sec 13
[5] Sec 15
[6] Sec 16
[7] Secs 17 and 18
[8] Sec 19 and following
[9] 24 and 25 Vict, Ch 100

Criminal Law Amendment Act, 1885,[1] or any offence under the Dangerous Performances Acts, 1879[2] and 1897[3] or an offence under the Children (Employment Abroad) Act, 1913,[4] or any offence involving bodily injury to a child or young person is committed.[5]

Powers of Constables.

The powers given in these cases are as follows—

A constable may take into custody, without warrant, any person—

(a) who within his view commits any of the offences enumerated, if the name and residence of such person are unknown to the constable and cannot be ascertained by him; or

(b) who has committed, or who the constable has reason to believe has committed, any such offence, if he has reasonable ground for believing that such person will abscond, or if the name and address of such person are unknown to and cannot be ascertained by the constable.

Bail to be Granted.

Where a constable arrests any person without warrant under this power the superintendent or inspector of police, or an officer of police of equal or superior rank, or the officer in charge of the police station to which such person is brought, shall, unless in his belief the release of such person on bail would tend to defeat the ends of justice, or to cause injury or danger to the child or young person against whom the offence is alleged to have been committed, release the person arrested on his entering into such a recognisance, with or without sureties, as may in the judgment of the officer of police be required to secure the attendance of such person upon the hearing of the charge.[6]

Detention of Child or Young Person in Place of Safety.

A constable, or any person authorised by a justice, may take to a place of safety any child or young person in respect of whom any offence above-mentioned has been, or there is reason to believe has been, committed

[1] 48 and 49 Vict., Ch. 69
[2] 42 and 43 Vict., Ch. 34
[3] 60 and 61 Vict., Ch. 52
[4] 3 and 4 Geo. V, Ch. 7
[5] Schedule 1, Children Act, 1908
[6] Sec. 19.

A child or young person so taken to a place of safety, and also any child or young person who seeks refuge in a place of safety, may there be detained until he can be brought before a Court of summary jurisdiction, and that Court may make such order for the care and detention of such child or young person, or may cause the child or young person to be dealt with as circumstances may admit or require, until the charge made against any person in respect of any offence as aforesaid with regard to the child or young person has been determined by the conviction or discharge of such person

Where it appears to a Court of summary jurisdiction or any justice that any such offence has been committed in respect of any child or young person who is brought before the Court or justice, and that it is expedient in the interests of the child or young person that an order should be made, the Court or justice may, without prejudice to any other power in the Children Act, make such order as circumstances require for the care and detention of the child or young person until a reasonable time has elapsed for a charge to be made against some person for having committed the offence If a charge is made against any person within that time, an order may be made for care and detention until the charge has been determined by the conviction or discharge of that person, and in case of conviction for such further time not exceeding twenty-one days as the Court which convicted may direct Any such order may be carried out notwithstanding that any person claims the custody of the child or young person [1]

Disposal of Child or Young Person by Order of the Court.

Where a person having the custody, charge, or care of a child or young person has been

(a) convicted of committing in respect of such child or young person any offence in question, or

(b) committed for trial for any such offence, or

(c) bound over to keep the peace towards such child or young person,

by any Court, that Court, either at the time when the person is so convicted, committed for trial, or bound over, and without requiring any new proceedings to be instituted for the purpose, or at any

[1] Sec 20

other time, and also any petty sessional Court before which any person may bring the case, may, if satisfied on enquiry that it is expedient so to deal with the child or young person, order that the child or young person be taken out of the custody, charge or care of the person so convicted, committed for trial, or bound over, and be committed to the care of a relative of the child or young person, or some other fit person named by the Court (such relative or other person being willing to undertake such care), until he attains the age of sixteen years, or for any shorter period Such Court or any Court of like jurisdiction may of its own motion, or on the application of any person, from time to time by order renew, vary and revoke any such order

When and How Made.

If any child or young person has a parent or legal guardian, no order shall be made unless the parent or legal guardian has been convicted of or committed to trial for the offence, or is under committal for trial for having been, or has been proved to the satisfaction of the Court making the order to have been, party or privy to the offence, or has been bound over to keep the peace towards the child or young person, or cannot be found

Every such order shall be in writing, and may be made by the Court in the absence of the child or young person, and the consent of any person to undertake the care of the child or young person in pursuance of any such order shall be proved in such manner as the Court may think sufficient to bind him

Where the order is made in respect of a person who has been committed for trial, then, if that person is acquitted of the charge, or if the charge is dismissed for want of prosecution, the order shall forthwith be void, except with regard to anything that may already have been lawfully done under it.

The Secretary of State may at any time in his discretion discharge a child or any young person from the care of any person to whose care he is committed in pursuance of this section, either absolutely or on such conditions as the Secretary of State approves, and may, if he thinks fit, make rules in relation to children or young persons so committed to the care of any person, and to the duties of such persons with respect to such children or young persons

The Secretary of State, in any case where it appears to him to be for the benefit of the child or young person who has been committed to the care of any person, may empower such person to procure the emigration of the child or young person, but, except with such authority, no person to whose care a child or young person is so committed shall procure his emigration.

The Court, instead of making such an order as respects a child, may order the child to be sent to an industrial school[1] in any case in which the Court is authorised to do so under Part IV of the Children Act.

Any person to whose care a child or young person is committed whilst the order is in force has the like control over the child or young person as if he were his parent, and shall be responsible for his maintenance, and the child or young person shall continue in the care of such person, notwithstanding that he is claimed by his parent or any other person, and if any person

(a) knowingly assists or induces, directly or indirectly, a child or young person to escape from the person to whose care he is so committed; or

(b) knowingly harbours, conceals, or prevents from returning to such person a child or young person who has so escaped, or knowingly assists in so doing,

he shall on summary conviction be liable to a fine not exceeding £20 or to be imprisoned, with or without hard labour, for any term not exceeding two months.

Maintenance of Child or Young Person.

Any Court having power so to commit any child or young person shall have power to make the like orders on the parent of or other person liable to maintain the child or young person, to contribute to his maintenance during such period as aforesaid, and such orders shall be enforceable in like manner as if the child or young person were ordered to be sent to a certified school under Part IV of the Children Act,[2] but the limit of the amount of the weekly sum which the parent or such person may be required under this section to contribute shall be £1 a week instead of the limit fixed under Part IV [3]

Any such order may be made on the complaint or application

---

[1] Sec 21 See Education, p 94   [2] *Infra*, p. 93 *et seq*
[3] That is, 5s per week

of the person to whose care the child or young person is for the time being committed, and either at the time when the order for the committal of the child or young person to his care is made, or subsequently, and the sums contributed by the parent or other such person shall be paid to such person as the Court may name, and be applied for the maintenance of the child or young person

When an order to commit a child or young person to the care of some relative or other person is made in respect of a person who has been committed for trial for an offence, the Court shall not have power to make an order on the parent or other person liable to maintain the child or young person prior to the trial of the person so committed

Attachment of Pensions.

Any Court making an order under this section for contribution by a parent or such other person may in any case where there is any pension or income payable to such parent or other person and capable of being attached, after giving the person by whom the pension or income is payable an opportunity of being heard, further order that such part as the Court may see fit of the pension or income be attached and be paid to the person named by the Court Such further order shall be an authority to the person by whom such pension or other income is payable to make the payment so ordered, and the receipt of the person to whom the payment is ordered to be made shall be a good discharge to such first-mentioned person

An order for contribution to maintenance may be made by any Court before which a person is charged with an offence of cruelty or other offence mentioned in the Children Act and the first schedule thereto, and without regard to the place in which the person to whom the payment is ordered to be made may reside.[1]

Religious Persuasion of Person to whom Child or Young Person is Committed.

In determining on the person to whose care the child or young person shall be committed, the Court shall endeavour to ascertain the religious persuasion to which the child or young person belongs, and shall, if possible, select a person of the same religious persuasion,

[1] Sec 22

or a person who gives such undertaking as seems to the Court sufficient that the child or young person shall be brought up in accordance with its own religious persuasion,[1] and such religious persuasion shall be specified in the order

In any case where the child or young person has been placed pursuant to any such order with a person who is not of the same religious persuasion as that to which the child or young person belongs, or who has not given such undertaking as aforesaid, the Court which made the order or any Court of like jurisdiction shall, on the application of any person in that behalf, and on its appearing that a fit person, who is of the same religious persuasion, or who will give such undertaking as aforesaid, is willing to undertake the care of the child or young person, make an order to secure his being placed with a person who either is of the same religious persuasion or gives such undertaking as aforesaid

Where a child or young person has been placed with a person who gives such undertaking as aforesaid, and the undertaking is not observed, the child or young person shall be deemed to have been placed with a person not of the same religious persuasion as that to which the child belongs, as if no such undertaking had been given [2]

Warrant to Search for or Remove Child or Young Person.

If it appears to a justice on information on oath laid by any person who, in the opinion of the justice, is acting in the interests of a child or young person, that there is reasonable cause to suspect

    (a) that the child or young person has been or is being assaulted, ill-treated, or neglected in any place within the jurisdiction of the justice, in a manner likely to cause the child or young person unnecessary suffering, or to be injurious to health ,

    (b) that any offence such as is under discussion [3] has been or is being committed in respect of the child or young person,

the justice may issue a warrant authorising any constable named therein to search for such child or young person, and if it is found that he has been or is being assaulted, illtreated, or neglected in manner aforesaid, or that any such offence has been or is being

---

[1] i e , usually its father's religion, see p 60   [2] Sec 23
[3] In the sections 12 to 18 of the Act and the first schedule thereto, see p 24

committed in respect of the child or young person, to take him to and detain him in a place of safety, until he can be brought before a Court of summary jurisdiction, or authorising any constable to remove the child or young person with or without search to a place of safety and detain him there until he can be brought before a Court of summary jurisdiction ; and the Court before whom the child or young person is brought may commit him to the care of a relative or other fit person in like manner as if the person in whose care he was had been committed for trial for such an offence

A justice issuing a warrant for this purpose may by the same warrant cause any person accused of any offence in respect of the child or young person to be apprehended and brought before a Court of summary jurisdiction, and proceedings to be taken against such person according to law

A constable authorised by warrant to search for any child or young person, or to remove any child or young person with or without search, may enter (if need be by force) any house, building, or other place specified in the warrant, and may remove the child or young person therefrom

Every such warrant issued shall be addressed to and executed by a constable who shall be accompanied by the person laying the information, if such person so desire, unless the justice by whom the warrant is issued otherwise directs, and may also, if the justice by whom the warrant is issued so directs, be accompanied by a duly qualified medical practitioner It is not necessary in any information or warrant to name the child or young person

Visitation of Homes.

The Secretary of State may cause any institution for the reception of poor children or young persons, supported wholly or partly by voluntary contributions, and not liable to be inspected by or under the authority of any Government Department, to be visited and inspected from time to time by persons appointed by him for the purpose

Any person so appointed shall have power to enter the institution, and any person who obstructs him in the execution of his duties shall be liable on summary conviction to a fine not exceeding £5, and a refusal to allow any person so appointed to enter the institution shall be deemed to be a reasonable cause to suspect that an offence is being committed in respect of a child or young person in the institution and a search warrant may be issued

Where an institution is carried on in accordance with the principles of any particular religious denomination, the Secretary of State shall, if so desired by the managers of the institution, appoint, where practicable, a person of that denomination to visit and inspect the institution, and in case the institution is for the reception of girls only, the Secretary of State shall, if so desired by the managers of the institution, appoint, where practicable, a woman to visit and inspect the institution. Appointments so made may at any time be revoked by the Secretary of State.[1]

Power as to Habitual Drunkards.

Where it appears to the Court by or before which any person is convicted of an offence of cruelty, or of any of the offences mentioned in the First Schedule to the Children Act, that that person is a parent of the child or young person in respect of whom the offence was committed, or is living with the parent of the child or young person, and is a habitual drunkard within the meaning of the Inebriates Acts, 1879[2] to 1900,[3] the Court in lieu of sentencing that person to imprisonment may, if it thinks fit, make an order for his detention in a retreat under the said Acts, the licensee of which is willing to receive him, for any period named in the order, not exceeding two years, and the order shall have the like effect, and copies thereof shall be sent to the local authority and Secretary of State in like manner, as if it were an application duly made by that person and duly attested by a justice under the said Acts, and the Court may order an officer of the Court or constable to remove that person to the retreat. On his reception in such retreat the said Acts shall have effect as if he had been admitted in pursuance of an application so made and attested as stated. Provided that—

 (a) an order for the detention of a person in retreat shall not be made unless that person, having had such notice as the Court thinks sufficient of the intention to allege habitual drunkenness, consents to the order being made; and

 (b) if the wife or husband of such person, being present at the

---

[1] Sec 25   [2] 42 and 43 Vict., Ch 19
[3] 51 and 52 Vict., Ch 19

hearing of the charge, objects to the order being made, the Court shall, before making the order, take into consideration any representation made to it by the wife or husband; and

(c) before making the order the Court shall, to such extent as it may deem reasonably sufficient, be satisfied that provision will be made for defraying the expenses of such person during detention in a retreat; and

(d) any power of the Court to order the person convicted to be detained in a certified inebriate reformatory is not affected.[1] An "habitual drunkard" is a person not being a lunatic who is, by reason of intemperance, dangerous to himself and others.[2]

Evidence of Accused Person.

Section 12 of the Prevention of Cruelty to Children Act, 1904, remains substantially unrepealed, hence in any proceeding against any person under that Act, such person shall be competent but not compellable to give evidence, and the wife or husband of such person may be required to attend to give evidence as an ordinary witness in the case, and shall be competent but not compellable to give evidence.[3]

The Children Act, 1908,[4] further provides that in any proceedings for any offence of cruelty under the Act or Schedule 1 of the Act[5] the Criminal Evidence Act, 1898,[6] shall apply in the same manner as if a reference to the Children Act, 1908, was substituted for the reference to the Prevention of Cruelty to Children Act, 1894.[7]

Power to take Deposition of Child or Young Person.

Where a justice is satisfied by the evidence of a duly qualified medical practitioner that the attendance before a Court of any child or young person, in respect of whom an offence under Part II of the Children Act,[8] or any of the offences mentioned in the First Schedule thereto,[9] is alleged to have been committed, would involve serious danger to the life or health of the child or young person, the justice may take in writing the deposition of the child or young person on oath, subscribe the deposition and add thereto a

---

[1] Sec 26
[2] 42 and 43 Vic, Ch 19, Sec 3
[3] 1 Ed VII, Ch 15, Sec 12
[4] 8 Ed VII, Ch 67, Sec 27
[5] Supra
[6] 61 and 62 Vict., Ch. 36
[7] 57 and 58 Vict, Ch. 41
[8] Sec. 12 et seq.
[9] See p 24.

statement of his reason for taking the deposition, and of the day when, and of the place where, the deposition was taken, and of the names of the persons (if any) present at the taking thereof

The justice taking such deposition shall transmit it with his statement to the proper officer of the Court for trial at which the accused person has been committed; and if he is not yet committed, to the Clerk of the Peace of the county or borough in which the deposition has been taken; and the Clerk of the Peace to whom any such deposition is transmitted shall preserve, file, and record the deposition.[1]

Admission of Deposition of Child or Young Person in Evidence.

If, on the trial of any person on indictment for any of the offences mentioned, the Court is satisfied by the evidence of a duly qualified medical practitioner that the attendance before the Court of any child or young person in respect of whom the offence is alleged to have been committed would involve serious danger to the life or health of the young person, any deposition of the child or young person taken under the Indictable Offences Act, 1848,[2] or taken as above, shall be admissible as evidence either for or against the accused person without further proof thereof if it purports to be signed by the justice by or before whom it purports to be taken; and if it is proved that reasonable notice in writing of the intention to take the deposition has been served[3] upon the person against whom it is proposed to use it as evidence, and that that person or his counsel or solicitor had, or might have had if he had chosen to be present, an opportunity of cross-examining the child or young person making the deposition

Evidence of Child of Tender Years.

If the child in respect of whom the offence is alleged to have been committed, or any other child of tender years who is tendered as a witness, does not, in the opinion of the Court, understand the nature of an oath, the evidence of that child may be received, though not given upon oath, if, in the opinion of the Court, the child is possessed of sufficient intelligence to justify the reception

[1] 8 Ed VII, Ch 67, Sec 28
[2] 11 and 12 Vict, Ch 42
[3] R v Shurmer, 17 Q B D 323, 55 L T R 126

of the evidence, and understands the duty of speaking the truth; and the evidence of the child, though not given on oath, but otherwise taken and reduced into writing in the form of depositions shall be deemed to be a deposition within the meaning of the foregoing provisions Provided that

(a) A person shall not be liable to be convicted of the offence unless the testimony admitted by virtue of this section and given on behalf of the prosecution is corroborated by some other material evidence in support thereof implicating the accused; and

(b) Any child, whose evidence is received as aforesaid and who wilfully gives false evidence under such circumstances that, if the evidence had been given on oath, he would have been guilty of perjury, shall, subject to the provisions of this Act, be liable on summary conviction to be adjudged such punishment as might have been awarded had he been charged with perjury and the case dealt with summarily under section 10 of the Summary Jurisdiction Act, 1879 [1]

If a child understands the nature of an oath, no corroborative evidence is necessary, and it is possible to obtain a conviction on the sworn evidence of the child How far the nature of an oath is understood by a child is a matter of fact He must at least know that he is under a higher duty than when merely relating to other persons what has occurred [2]

Power to Proceed with Case in Absence of Child or Young Person.

If the Court is satisfied that the attendance before the Court of any child or young person in respect of whom the offence is alleged to have been committed is not essential to the just hearing of the case, the case may be proceeded with and determined in the absence of the child or young person [3]

Mode of Charging Offences and Limitation of Time.

Where a person is charged with committing an offence in respect of two or more children or young persons, the same information or summons may charge the offence in respect of all or any of them,

---

[1] 42 and 43 Vict, Ch 49
[2] *Rex* v *Dent*, 71 J P 511
[3] Sec 31, Children Act, 1908

but the person charged shall not be liable to a separate penalty for each child or young person except upon separate informations.

The same information or summons may also charge any person as having the custody, charge or care, alternatively or together, and may charge him with the offences of assault, ill-treatment, neglect, abandonment, or exposure, together or separately, and may charge him with committing all or any of these offences in a manner likely to cause unnecessary suffering or injury to health, alternatively or together, but when these offences are charged together the person charged shall not be liable to a separate penalty for each.

A person shall not be summarily convicted of an offence under Part II of the Children Act, or of an offence mentioned in the First Schedule thereto, unless the offence was wholly or partly committed within six months before the information was laid, but, subject as aforesaid, evidence may be taken of acts constituting or contributing to constitute the offence, and committed at any previous time

When an offence is a continuous offence, it shall not be necessary to specify in the information, summons, or indictment, the date of the acts constituting the offence [1]

Appeal from Summary Conviction to Quarter Sessions.

Any person convicted by a Court of summary jurisdiction of an offence, or when in the case of any application to a Court of summary jurisdiction for an order committing a child or young person to the care of any person, or for an order for contribution to the maintenance of a child or young person any party thereto, thinking himself aggrieved by any order or decision of the Court, may appeal against such a conviction, or order, or decision to quarter sessions.[2]

Institution of Proceedings by Guardian, etc.

A board of guardians may institute any proceedings for any offence[3] in relation to a child or young person, and may, out of their common fund, pay the reasonable costs and expenses of any proceedings so instituted by them.

[1] Sec 32. [2] Sec 33. [3] Under the Children Act, Part II

The like powers of instituting proceedings may, in London, be also exercised by the County Council except in the City where the Common Council acts, and the expenses of such proceedings shall be defrayed as expenses of the authority out of the County Fund or general rates.[1]

[1] Secs. 34 and 10, Children Act, 1908

CHAPTER III

INFANT LIFE PROTECTION AND MISCELLANEOUS MATTERS

Many Acts of Parliament have been aimed at the checking of infantile mortality. On perusing the Forty-second Annual Report of the Local Government Board, we note that a variety of legislative enactments are mentioned which have been of some service in this respect. Among these may be cited the Notification of Births Act, 1907.[1] Modern industrial conditions are such that it is quite impossible to account for changes that have taken place in this respect. According to the Report, weather conditions would seem to play an important part in the figures stated. In industrial areas where infant labour was formerly employed, the provisions of the Factory Acts and various other enactments in relation to women's and children's employment have had considerable effect, both on the birth rate and on infantile mortality. A large amount of female labour is employed in these localities, and the neglect of home ties by women who are forced to work has a material influence over the birth rate. It is very difficult to decide what is the cause of many of the fluctuations in the figures noted in the report, but certainly modern legislation has a great deal to do with this matter. Among some of the more important of the enactments are the provisions of the Children Act, preventing what is popularly known as "baby-farming." The following are the chief protective provisions in that Act—

Notices to be given by Persons Receiving Infants for Reward.

Where a person undertakes for reward for a period of over forty-eight hours, the nursing and maintenance of one or more infants under the age of seven years apart from their parents or having no parents, he or she shall give notice in writing to the local authority within forty-eight hours from the reception of any such infant.

If a person undertakes for reward the nursing and maintenance

[1] 7 Ed. VII, Ch. 40.

of an infant already in his care without reward, the entering into the undertaking is to be treated as a reception of the infant.

The notice to the local authority must state the name, sex, and date and place of birth of the infant, the name of the person receiving the infant, and the dwelling within which the infant is being kept, and the name and address of the person from whom the infant has been received

If a person who has undertaken the nursing and maintenance of any such infant changes his residence, he shall give to the local authority notice in writing of the change within forty-eight hours thereof, and where the residence to which he moves is situate in the district of another local authority, he shall in respect of each infant in his care give to that local authority a notice similar to the one required to be given on the first reception of the infant

If any such infant dies, or is removed from the care of the person who has undertaken its nursing and maintenance, that person shall give to the local authority notice in writing of the death or removal within forty-eight hours thereof, and in the latter case also of the address and name of the person to whose care the infant has been transferred

If any person required to give a notice fails to give the notice within the time specified for giving the notice, he is guilty of an offence under the Children Act, and if the infant in respect of which notice ought to have been given was an infant the consideration for whose nursing and maintenance consisted in whole or in part of a lump sum, the person failing to give the notice shall in addition to any other penalty be liable to forfeit that sum or such less sum as the Court having cognizance of the case may deem just, and the sum forfeited shall be applied for the benefit of the infant in such manner as the Court may direct, and where any such sum is ordered to be forfeited the order may be enforced as if it were an order of the Court made on complaint.[1]

Appointment and Powers of Inspectors, etc.

It is the duty of every local authority to provide for the carrying out of the law in this respect within their district, and for that purpose they shall from time to time make enquiry whether there are any persons residing therein who undertake the nursing and

[1] See Children Act, 1908, Sec 1 (7)

maintenance of infants in respect of whom notice is required to be given.

If, in the district of any local authority, any persons are found who undertake the nursing and maintenance of such infants as aforesaid, the local authority shall appoint one or more persons of either sex to be infant protection visitors, whose duty it shall be from time to time to visit any infants referred to in any notice given, and the premises in which they are kept, in order to satisfy themselves as to the proper nursing and maintenance of the infant, or to give any necessary advice or directions as to their nursing and maintenance, but the local authority may, either in addition to or in lieu of appointing infant protection visitors, authorise in writing one or more suitable persons of either sex to exercise the powers of infant protection visitors subject to such terms and conditions as may be stated in the authorisation, and where any infants have been placed out to nurse in the district of the authority by any philanthropic society may, if satisfied that the interests of the infants are properly safeguarded, so authorise the society to exercise those powers as respects those infants, subject, however, to the obligation to furnish periodical reports to the local authority

A local authority may combine with any other local authority for the purpose of executing the provisions of this part of the Children Act, and for defraying the expenses thereof

A local authority may exempt from being visited, either unconditionally or subject to such conditions as they think fit, any particular premises within their district which appear to them to be so conducted that it is unnecessary that they should be visited

If any person undertaking the nursing and maintenance of any such infants refuses to allow any such visitor or other person to visit or examine the infants or the premises in which they are kept, he shall be guilty of an offence under the Children Act

If any such visitor or other person is refused admittance to any premises, or has reason to believe that any infants under the age of seven years are being kept in any house or premises in contravention of the Children Act, he may apply to a justice who, on being satisfied on information in writing on oath that there is reasonable grounds for believing that such an offence has been committed, may grant a warrant authorising the visitor or other person to enter the premises for the purpose of ascertaining whether any such offence has been committed, and if the occupier of the premises or any other person obstructs, or causes or procures to be obstructed, any visitor or other person acting in pursuance of such a warrant, he shall be guilty of an offence under the Children Act.[1]

Persons Prohibited from Receiving Children for Reward.

An infant in respect of which notice is required to be given shall not, without the written sanction of the local authority, be kept—

(a) by any person from whose care any infant has been removed under this part of the Children Act or under the Infant Life Protection Act, 1897 ; or

(b) in any premises from which any infant has been removed by reason of the premises being dangerous or insanitary, or has been removed under the Infant Life Protection Act, 1897, by reason of the premises being so unfit as to endanger its health ; or

(c) by any person who has been convicted of any offence under Part II of the Children Act or under the Prevention of Cruelty to Children Act, 1904 ;

and any person keeping, or causing to be kept, an infant contrary to this section shall be guilty of an offence under the Children Act.[2]

Local Authority to Fix Number of Infants which may be Retained.

The local authority may fix the number of infants under the age of seven years which may be kept in any dwelling in respect of which a notice has been received, and any person keeping any infant in excess of the number so fixed shall be guilty of an offence.[3]

Removal of Infant Improperly Kept.

If any infant, in respect of which notice is required to be given, is kept—

(a) in any premises which are overcrowded, dangerous or insanitary, or

(b) by any person who, by reason of negligence, ignorance, inebriety, immorality, criminal conduct, or other similar cause, is unfit to have care of it ; or

(c) by any person, or in any premises in contravention of any of the provisions of the Children Act,[4]

any visitor or other person appointed or authorised to execute

---

[1] Sec. 2, Part 1 [2] Sec. 3. [3] Sec. 4 [4] Part 1

the provisions of Part I of the Children Act may apply either to a justice or to the local authority for an order directing him to remove the infant to a place of safety until it can be restored to its relatives or be otherwise lawfully disposed of.

Any person refusing to comply with an order upon its being produced and read over to him, or obstructing or causing or procuring to be obstructed, the visitor or other person in the execution thereof, shall be guilty of an offence under Part I of the Children Act, and

(a) if the order was made by a justice, the order may be enforced by the visitor or by any constable; and

(b) if the order was made by the local authority, the visitor or other person may apply to any justice for an order directing the removal of the infant, which order may be enforced by the visitor or by any constable.[1]

Notice to Coroner.

In the case of the death of any infant respecting which notice is required to be given, the person who had the care of the infant shall, within twenty-four hours of the death, give notice in writing thereof to the coroner of the district within which the body of the infant lies, and the coroner shall hold an inquest thereon, unless a certificate under the hand of a duly qualified medical practitioner is produced to him, certifying that he has personally attended the infant during its last illness, and specifying the cause of death, and the coroner is satisfied that there is no ground for holding an inquest

If any person required to give a notice under this section fails to give the notice within the time specified, he shall be guilty of an offence under Part I of the Children Act [2]

Avoidance of Policies of Life Insurance of Infants kept for Reward. 14 Geo. III, c. 48.

A person by whom an infant in respect of which notice is required to be given is kept shall be deemed to have no interest in the life of the child for the purpose of the Life Assurance Act, 1774, and if any such person directly or indirectly insures, or attempts to insure the life of such an infant, he shall be guilty of an offence under Part I of the Children Act, and if a company within the meaning

---

[1] Sec. 5.   [2] Sec 6

of the Life Assurance Companies Acts, 1870 to 1872, or any other company, society or person knowingly issues, or procures, or attempts to procure to be issued to or for the benefit of such a person as aforesaid, or to any person on his behalf, a policy on the life of such an infant, the company, society or person shall be guilty of an offence under Part I.[1]

Provisions as to Notices.

If any person required to give a notice knowingly or wilfully makes, or causes or procures any other person to make, any false or misleading statements in any such notice, he shall be guilty of an offence under Part I.

Every notice required to be given may be sent by post in a registered letter addressed to the clerk of the local authority, or to such other person as the local authority may appoint, or it may be delivered at the office of the local authority, or, in the case of a notice to a coroner, to the coroner at his office or residence.[2]

Prosecution of Offences and Application of Fines.

Every person guilty of an offence under Part I of the Children Act shall, on summary conviction, be liable to imprisonment for a term not exceeding six months, or to a fine not exceeding £25, and the Court may order any infant in respect of which the offence was committed to be removed to a place of safety

Any fines recovered under the Children Act, Part I, notwithstanding any provision in any other Act, shall be paid to the local authority and be applied to the purposes to which the fund or rate out of which the expenses of the local authority are to be defrayed is applicable[3]

Local Authorities and Expenses.

The local authority for the purposes of Part I of the Children Act, shall—

    (a) as respects the County of London, exclusive of the City, be the county council;
    (b) as respects the City of London, be the common council;
    (c) elsewhere be the guardians of the poor law union

---

[1] Sec 7   [2] Sec 8   [3] Sec 9

All expenses incurred by and on behalf of the local authority shall be defrayed—

(a) in the case of the county of London, out of the county fund as general county expenses;

(b) in the case of the City of London, out of the general rate;

(c) in the case of the board of guardians, out of the common fund.[1]

Exemptions.

The above provisions respecting custody of infants shall not extend to any relative or legal guardian of an infant who undertakes the nursing and maintenance of the infant, or to any person who undertakes the nursing or maintenance of an infant under the provisions of any Act for the relief of the poor, or of any order made under any such Act, or to hospitals, convalescent homes, or institutions established for the protection and care of infants, and conducted in good faith for religious or charitable purposes, or boarding schools at which efficient elementary education is provided.

For the purposes of this section the expression "relatives" means grandparents, brothers, sisters, uncles, and aunts, by consanguinity or affinity, and in the case of illegitimate infants the persons who would be so related if the infant were legitimate.[2]

Miscellaneous.

A peculiar kind of protection is provided in the miscellaneous provisions of the Children Act, 1908.[3] These provisions, together with recent decisions of the Courts, give adequate protection against accident to children at places of entertainment and in schools.

Safety of Places of Entertainment.

Where an entertainment for children, or an entertainment where the majority of those attending are children, is provided, care must be taken for the safety of those present. If the number of children attending exceeds 100, and access to the place of entertainment is by stairs, it is the duty of those providing the entertainment to station, and to keep stationed wherever necessary, a sufficient number of adult attendants, properly instructed as to

[1] Sec. 10   [2] Sec. 11   [3] Sec. 121.

their duties, to prevent more children or other persons being admitted to any such part of the building than that part can properly accommodate, and to control the movement of the children and other persons admitted to any such part whilst entering and leaving, and to take all other reasonable precautions for the safety of the children

The occupier of the building letting the building for reward is also under a duty to see that the provisions of the law, as above stated, are complied with.

Penalty.

Failure to comply with the law in this respect is visited with a penalty not exceeding £50 for a first offence on summary conviction, and £100 for a second or subsequent offence. If the premises are licensed as a theatre, or for music or dancing, a second conviction may entail a revocation of the licence by the authority which granted it.

Proceedings.

If the building is licensed by the Lord Chamberlain, the county or county borough council, in which the building is situated, are under a duty to take proceedings where the law is broken, and the police are to institute proceedings if the licence was granted by the county or county borough council

A constable may enter any building in which he has reason to believe that a children's entertainment is being, or about to be provided, with a view to seeing whether the proper precautions are being taken

If the place of entertainment is a private dwelling-house the provision does not apply

The law is extremely vague, and no doubt difficulties of construction may arise. As to what number of adult persons will be sufficient to act as attendants, and what instructions are proper instructions as to their duties, these are questions of fact which may prove difficult to determine. It may also be questioned whether a constable is a sufficiently expert person to determine whether the provisions of the law are complied with. The most important and perhaps the most adequate part of the enactment is the licence control specifically provided

46 THE CHILD: ITS PROTECTION, EDUCATION, EMPLOYMENT

Injury in School.

During recent years several decisions have been reported which indicate that the duty cast upon a local education authority to provide and maintain, and keep efficient all the public elementary schools within their area,[1] includes a duty to safeguard any child in attendance from accidents due to imperfections in buildings. The cases have gone much further than this, and have cast an almost absolute duty upon the local authority to guard children from injury.

Ching v. Surrey County Council.

In *Ching v. Surrey County Council*[2] the plaintiff, suing by his father as next friend, claimed damages against the defendants for injuries suffered through their negligence. The plaintiff was a pupil at a public elementary school provided by the defendants.

While lawfully playing in the playground, the plaintiff caught his foot in a hole and was injured. At the trial the jury gave a verdict for the plaintiff for £83 19s 6d, and Mr Justice Bucknill held that the defendants were liable. In supporting this decision, Lord Halsbury said—

"I think the words 'maintain and keep efficient' applicable to a school must necessarily mean not only what has been described as the scholastic system which is to be enforced, but also refer to the question as to when, where, or how the duty is to be performed by those who are under the main duty of keeping the school efficient for the scholars . . . that is to say, keeping it fit in respect to health, comfort, and so on, and all that which is necessarily involved in saying that you should keep school children in a place which it is fit for them to be in."[3]

The decision of the Court of Appeal in *Ching v. Surrey County Council* was followed in *Morris v. Carnarvon County Council*[4] where the plaintiff, a girl six years of age, was a pupil at a school under the defendants' control. Two of the schoolrooms were connected by a heavy door which swung in both directions and was controlled by a strong spring. The door had been erected before the school passed under the defendants' control and had not been

---

[1] Education Act, 1902, 2 Ed VII, Ch 42, Sec 7 (1)
[2] Court of Appeal, 1910, 1 K B 736, 102 L T R 414
[3] Per Lord Halsbury, 102 L T R, pp 416 and 417.
[4] (Court of Appeal) (1910) 1 K.B 840 and 102 L T R 524.

interfered with by them. Upon the 4th of November, 1908, the plaintiff was late for school and passed through the swing door, contrary to instructions to late arrivals, into a room where her classmates were attending the call of registers. She was told to retire by a mistress, and in passing through the swing door, without assistance, one of her fingers was injured by the door swinging back. The finger had to be amputated. The plaintiff sued the defendants for damages, and at the trial the jury found that the defendants were guilty of negligence in allowing the door to remain as it was, and also that the door, as originally constructed, was not suitable for infants.

Upon these findings the learned judge entered judgment for the plaintiff, and his decision was upheld on appeal. It was laid down that the duties taken over by the defendants were not merely as to scholastic matters, but also duties relating to the physical condition of the school; that there was a duty on the defendants to discover the danger of the door and to substitute a safer means of access to the schoolroom, and that the defendants not having performed that duty were liable to the plaintiff in damages.

Shrimpton v. Herefordshire County Council.

The liability of an education authority extends beyond these principles, and includes the common law liability that where a person provides anything for the use of another, he is bound to provide a thing reasonably safe for the purpose for which it is intended, even though the person using it uses it only by the permission or consent of the person providing it and has no legal claim to the use of it.[1]

Where an education authority, in pursuance of their statutory powers,[2] provided a vehicle to convey certain children who lived at a distance, to and from their school, and a child who lived nearer to the school and was not one of those for whom the vehicle was provided, was conveyed in it with the consent of the education authority, and while getting out of it fell and was injured in consequence of there being no attendant in addition to the driver to help the children to get in and out, it was held, reversing the judgment in the Court of Appeal, that there was evidence of negligence on the

---

[1] *Shrimpton v. Hereford County Council* (H of L), 101 L.T.R. 145
[2] Education (Admins Prov) Act, 1907, 7 Ed. VII, Ch 43, Sec 14

part of the education authority and that they were liable for the child's injury.

Smith v. Martin and the Mayor, etc., of Kingston-upon-Hull.

These foregoing decisions have had an influence on the decision of the Court of Appeal in *Smith v. Martin and the Mayor, etc., of Kingston-upon-Hull*,[1] where the facts were rather dissimilar and turned on the liability of a master for the acts of a servant.

In this case the plaintiff, a girl of fourteen years of age, a pupil at a public elementary school, was sent by her teacher to poke the fire and draw out the damper in a room used by the teachers for their own convenience. In the course of obeying this order her pinafore caught fire and she was burnt and injured.

In an action brought by her against the teacher and the defendant corporation, who were the local education authority, claiming damages in respect of her injuries, the jury awarded plaintiff £300 damages. It was held that the teacher was liable, and that the relation of the education authority to the teacher was that of master and servant, so that the principle *qui facit per alium facit per se* upon which the master is made responsible for the act or omission of his servant, was applicable, and further that the direction given by the teacher to the plaintiff was not outside the scope of her employment, so that the education authority were responsible for the direction given by her.

Farwell, L.J.

In his judgment in this case Lord Justice Farwell's[2] remarks on the position of teacher and pupil are worthy of note.

"In my opinion the Education Acts are intended to provide for education in its truest and widest sense; such education includes the inculcation of habits of order, obedience, and courtesy; such habits are taught by giving orders, and if such orders are reasonable and proper under the circumstances of the case, they are within the scope of the teacher's authority even although they are not confined to bidding the child read or write, to sit down or to stand up in school, or the like. It would be extravagant to say that a teacher has no business to ask a child to perform small acts of courtesy to herself or others, such as to fetch her pocket-handkerchief from upstairs, to poke the fire in the teachers' room, or to

[1] (Court of Appeal) (1911), 2 K B 775, and 105 L T R 281
[2] 105 L T R at p 285.

open the door for a visitor, or the like. It is said that these are for the teacher's own benefit, but I do not agree; not only is it good for the child to be taught to be unselfish and obliging, but the opportunity of running upstairs may often avoid punishment; the wise teacher who sees a volatile child becoming fidgety may well make the excuse of an errand for herself an outlet for the child's exuberance of spirits, very much to the benefit of the child. Teachers must use their common sense, and it would be disastrous to hold that they can do nothing but teach. Then it is suggested that the acts in this case cannot be for the master's benefit. I have recently delivered a judgment[1] on this point and I will not repeat it; it is enough to say now that ' benefit ' does not mean ' pecuniary benefit ' only; an act done within the scope of employment is, by legal intendment, for the benefit of the master, unless and until the master proves the contrary."

It will be seen, therefore, that children are very adequately protected from injury during the time that they are in school or lawfully on the school premises or *semble* even whilst off the school premises in obedience to orders of a teacher.

[1] *Lloyd v. Grace, Smith & Co.* (1911), 2 K.B. 489; 104 L.T.R. 789

CHAPTER IV

CUSTODY AND MAINTENANCE OF INFANTS

THE wardship of infants and their religious education are subjects very closely connected, but as it is desirable to treat of the question of religious education in a separate chapter,[1] this aspect will be ignored at this point except where it is so closely allied to the wardship of infants that such an attitude is impossible. To this extent the chapters may be found to overlap.

We shall not in this chapter approach the matter of custody from the point of view of the Children Act, 1908,[2] or the Employment of Children Act, 1903,[3] which Acts provide for the removal of children from parental control in certain cases.[4]

Father's Common Law Right.

Under the common law of England the rights of parents are not co-equal. The father is deemed to have the pre-eminent right to control his infant children although as to illegitimate children the mother is the natural guardian.[5] The chief limitation placed upon the father's right is that in general the power of the Chancery Division is paramount, but will only be exercised in derogation of the father's right when such exercise is for the infant's benefit.

Although the common law rule is quite clear and precise it does not contain all that may be said on the question of guardianship and custody of infants. Various enactments provide for various contingencies. These may be divided into three classes. Firstly, those providing for custody when the question is raised as an issue in matrimonial disputes or difficulties. Secondly, those extending or rather supplying the missing common law rights of the mother. And thirdly, the enactments providing for the guardianship after the father's death.

Questions of matrimonial causes will be treated of later in this chapter,[6] and our present object will be to discuss the mother's

---

[1] See p. 60 et seq.   [2] 8 Ed. VII, Ch. 67, Sec. 21
[3] 3 Ed. VII, Ch. 45, Sec. 5 (4)   [4] See Infra
[5] Barnardo v. McHugh (1891), A.C. 388   [6] p. 53

rights and the various forms of guardianship other than that of father and mother.

Guardianship of Infants Act, 1886, Sec. 5.

The greatest inroad upon the common law rights of the father during the father's lifetime and apart from the provisions of the law as administered in the Probate, Divorce and Admiralty Division, is made by the Guardianship of Infants Act, 1886,[1] which provides as follows—

"The Court may, upon the application of the mother of any infant (who may apply without next friend), make such order as it may think fit regarding the custody of such infant and the right of access thereto of either parent, having regard to the welfare of the infant, and to the conduct of the parents, and to the wishes as well of the mother as of the father, and may alter, vary, or discharge such order on the application of either parent, or, after the death of either parent, of any guardian under this Act, and in every case may make such order respecting the costs of the mother and the liability of the father for the same, or otherwise as to costs as it may think just."

This section of the Act confers a very wide discretion upon the Court, a discretion far wider than that given in the Custody of Infants Act, 1873[2] or in the earlier Talfourd's Act.[3] The Act of 1886 will not, however, be applied where an order as to custody has been made in a matrimonial suit in the Divorce Court.[4] The Divorce Court in exercising its right to make an order as to custody acts on its own discretion,[5] but in so acting it is governed by the circumstances of the case and *has special regard to the father's common law right*. On the other hand, the Chancery Division in the exercise of its right under the Guardianship of Infants Act, 1886, has the widest discretion and will more easily override the rule that the custody and control of a child resides in the father.[6] The points the Court has regard to are "(1) the welfare of the infant, (2) the conduct of the parents, and (3) the wishes as well of the mother as of the father." These also seem to have been the points which influenced the Divorce Court in *Mozley Stark v. Mozley*

---

[1] 49 and 50 Vict., Ch. 27, Sec. 5   [2] 36 and 37 Vict., Ch. 12
[3] 2 and 3 Vict., Ch. 54
[4] *Manders v. Manders*, 63, L.T. 627   [5] See p. 55
[6] *In re A and B (Infants)* (1897), 1 Ch. D. 786

Stark.[1] The Chancery Division will treat the parents equally and take the conduct and wishes of each into consideration, giving the custody of infant children to the mother despite her matrimonial misconduct, if in the opinion of the Court the case is a proper one for such order to be made.[2]

In *In re A and B (Infants)* in the Court of Appeal, Rigby L.J.,[3] reviewed the sections of the Guardianship of Infants Act, 1886, with the object of showing that the sole intention of the legislature was to give new and important rights to the mother not equal rights with the father over the whole field of guardianship for by section 2, only on the father's death, the mother becomes guardian either solely or jointly with any guardian appointed by the father.[4] By section 3 the mother may appoint a guardian to act after the death of herself and the father.[5]

It has been argued that the rights of the father are rights for his own benefit, but it is now quite settled that they are for the infants' benefit.[6] This is reiterated in section 5[7] of the Guardianship of Infants Act, 1886. It is therein stated that the Court must have regard "to the welfare of the infant," and Rigby, L.J.,[8] suggests that the appearance of this point first in the section makes it impossible to say that the rights of the father are to be the first consideration of the Court. Without this close reasoning the whole of the section is opposed to the view that you must first look to the rights of the father. Nothing may be read into an Act of Parliament save the actual words present. It is the duty of the Court to interpret the meaning of the words, and the Court in the case above cited, refused to interpret the meaning of the phrase "the wishes as well of the mother as of the father" as being equal to the wishes of the mother without prejudice to the rights of the father at common law, and as they stand by the decisions down to this time.[9] Providing that the conduct of both parents is taken into consideration, misconduct on the part of the wife will not necessarily bind the Court to refuse her an order.[10] In *In re A and B*[11] it was decided that notwithstanding the wife's misconduct condoned

---

[1] (1910) P. 190, see p. 54
[2] (1897), 1 Ch. D. 786
[3] (1897) 1 Ch. D. 792
[4] See p. 53
[5] See p. 53
[6] (1910) 101 L.T.R. at p. 771 and (1894) P. 305
[7] q.v., p. 51
[8] (1897) 1 Ch. D. 793
[9] (1897) 1 Ch. D. 795
[10] See *Divorce*, p. 55
[11] (1897) 1 Ch. 786

by the husband and the fact that the wife had had a period of intemperance, she was not to be deprived of her rights to an order under the section, the husband having also been guilty of misconduct condoned by the wife. It was provided that each party should have the custody for six months in the year, provision being made for education and also for the protection of the children whilst in their mother's care.

The Mother as Guardian.

Provision is made in the Guardianship of Infants Act, 1886, for the mother to become guardian after her husband's death. At common law she became "guardian by nurture" but not during full minority and only in default of guardians appointed by the father under 12 Car. II, Ch. 24. The widow's common law guardianship of her sons extended to the sons' fourteenth year and of daughters to the sixteenth year, but under the Act of 1886 the widowed mother becomes statutory guardian either solely or jointly with a guardian appointed by the father.

Where the mother becomes sole guardian the Court may appoint a joint guardian in case of necessity [1] or even remove her from the guardianship.

Guardian Appointed by Mother.

By the Guardianship of Infants Act,[2] section 3, the mother may appoint a guardian for her children. Such appointment may be by deed or by will, and the guardian so appointed acts after the death of both parents, jointly with any guardian appointed by the father.

Where the father is unfitted to act as guardian, the mother may appoint a guardian to act with the father after her death, but it is necessary in such case for the appointment to be confirmed by the Court.

Something more will be said as to guardianship and maintenance after examining the position of the father and mother in relation to the children in matrimonial causes.

Powers of P.D.A. as to Custody.

Although the care and custody of children are matters over which

---

[1] *In re Scanlon*, 40 Ch. D. 200 but see *In re X v Y* (1899), 1 Ch. 526
[2] 49 and 50 Vict., Ch. 27, Sec. 3

the Chancery division has cognisance, we must not lose sight of the fact that the Probate, Divorce and Admiralty Division of the High Court must play a not insignificant part in such matters The Matrimonial Causes Acts of 1857,[1] 1859,[2] and 1884,[3] respectively, make provision for the custody, maintenance, and education of children affected by decisions of the Court in matrimonial causes. Thus the Probate, Divorce, and Admiralty Division has power either in separation, nullity, dissolution, or restitution suits, to make provision for the custody, maintenance, and education of the children of a marriage

This jurisdiction does not cease when the child attains the age of sixteen,[4] but it exists throughout the child's minority except that as Lord Lindley in his judgment in *Thomasset* v. *Thomasset*[5] said, " I do not say that a child who has attained years of discretion can, except under very special circumstances, be properly ordered into the custody of either parent against such child's own wishes "[6] In such " special circumstances " it would be usual to make the child a ward of Court, so putting the machinery of the Chancery Division in motion for the child's benefit

As is pointed out in the chapter on " Religious Education,"[7] the rights of custody and control are for the child's benefit and not for the benefit of the parent,[8] the child's welfare is paramount, and a child having reached years of discretion may be allowed by the Court to remain in the custody of a guilty parent [9] In the written judgment of the Court of Appeal in *Mozley Stark* v *Mozley Stark* the Master of Rolls said—

" That the matrimonial offence which justified divorce ought not to be regarded for all time and under all circumstances as sufficient to disentitle the mother to access to her daughter or even to the custody of her daughter assuming her to be under sixteen The Court ought not to lay down a hard and fast rule on this subject. The statutory power conferred upon the Court ought in the

---

[1] 20 and 21 Vict , Ch 85, Sec 35
[2] 22 and 23 Vict , Ch 61, Sec 44
[3] 47 and 48 Vict , Ch 68, Sec 6
[4] *Thomasset* v *Thomasset*, 71 L T R 148 and (1894), P 295
[5] (1894), P 302
[6] See *Queen* v *Gyngall* (1893), 2 Q B at p 251, as to the Chancery Division's attitude towards children since Judicature Act, 1873
[7] Infra, p 60   [8] See p 52
[9] *Mozley Stark* v *Mozley Stark* (now *Hitchins*) and *Hitchins*, 1910 (Ct of App), 101 L T R , p 770 , (1910) P 190

language of Lopes, L.J, in *Thomasset* v. *Thomasset*[1] 'to be exercised at the discretion of the Court according to the particular circumstances in each case in which its interference is invoked' And it is always to be borne in mind that the benefit and interest of the infant is the paramount consideration and not the punishment of the guilty spouse."[2]

In all cases it will be seen that the Court exercises its powers in a discretionary manner, being guided by the circumstances and always having regard to the father's common law rights. Children of tender years will as a rule be left with the mother[3] if their health depends upon such course. The guilty party is not usually entitled to custody, but in cases custody has been given to a guilty husband[4] and more rarely to a guilty wife.[5]

Giving Access.

The party to whom custody is granted may be ordered to give access to the other party at stated times, but such an order will not usually be made in favour of a guilty wife although it often is made in favour of a guilty husband

Orders, How Obtained.

An order for custody will not be made unless the petition asks for one. Applications for custody should be made by summons supported by affidavit to a judge in chambers if the final decree in a suit makes no provision. Access can be obtained by summons to a registrar who has a discretionary power which is subject to appeal to the Court.

Under the Summary Jurisdiction (Married Women) Act, 1895,[6] justices have power to make an order as to the custody of children under sixteen. Such legal custody is given to the wife where she has not been guilty of adultery.

The Guardianship of Infants Act, 1886,[7] provides that the guilty party in a divorce or separation suit may, after the decree, be declared to be unfit to have the custody of the children of the marriage and that on the death of the innocent parent the right to custody or guardianship shall not pass to the guilty one. The offence, however, does not affect the party for all time so that a

---

[1] (1894) P 305
[2] 101 L J R , p 771
[3] *Barnes* v *Barnes*, 1 P and D 463
[4] *Martin* v *Martin*, 2 L T 188
[5] *Pryor* v *Pryor* (1900), P 157
[6] 58 and 59 Vict , Ch 39
[7] 49 and 50 Vict , Ch 27 Sec 7

future application for custody might well be entertained on proof of good conduct

Testamentary Guardian.

At common law the father's right to the control of his children terminated at his death, but by the Statute of Military Tenures[1] the father was allowed by deed or will to appoint a guardian to protect and govern his infant children. Such guardian is generally known as a testamentary guardian. Under the Guardianship of Infants Act, 1886, as we have already seen, a mother has now a similar right of appointing a guardian to her surviving infant children.[2]

Guardian appointed by the Court.

Where neither father nor mother has exercised his or her statutory right to appoint a guardian, as, for example, where a father dies under the age of twenty-one not having executed a deed appointing a guardian under 12 Car. 2, Ch. 24, the Court would make an appointment in a proper case, since any will made by the father, a minor, would be inoperative. The jurisdiction of the Court arises from the Court's authority as delegate of the Crown to act as guardian over all infants.[3]

Removal of a Guardian by the Court.

Under the exercise of this jurisdiction, the Chancery Division may, when necessary to the infant's welfare, remove a guardian from his office, and, incidentally, appoint another person to fill his place. This power applies where the guardian was originally appointed by the Court or where the guardian is a testamentary guardian appointed by the father or the mother under the Guardianship of Infants Act, 1886.

Wards of Court.

Where the Court interferes in the guardianship of an infant and appoints or removes a guardian, the infant is generally considered to be a ward of Court, but it is not necessary for the Court to appoint a guardian in order that the position of ward of Court may be created. An infant becomes a ward of Court when any action respecting an infant's person or property is commenced in the

[1] 12 Car. 2, Ch. 24 [2] See p. 53
[3] *Queen v. Gyngall* (1893), 2 Q.B., 232 *et seq.*

Chancery Division It is often stated that when an infant becomes a ward of Court he must have property This is not essentially necessary theoretically, but in practice the Court only exercises jurisdiction where protection is required for property, or the infant has property which can be administered by the Court for the infant's benefit.

Whenever an application is made to the Court for maintenance, the infant in respect of whom such application is made becomes a ward of Court, and in the cases where a petition is presented under the Custody of Infants Act, 1873,[1] an order made upon such petition would cause the infant to become a ward of Court Applications for maintenance are made by summons at Chambers.

Duties of Guardian.

A guardian has a right to the custody and care of an infant over whom he exercises jurisdiction He has control over the education and place of residence of his ward, except that in the case of a ward of Court he may not remove the person of the ward out of the jurisdiction of the Court without the Court's consent. He has a right to regulate the education of his ward, subject to the limitation that the religious education must be in accordance with the wishes of the father, or if no such wishes have been expressed, must be in accordance with the father's religion.[2] The authority of the guardian extends not only to the person of the ward, but also to the ward's property In this matter, therefore, the guardian is a trustee and must account to his ward when the ward comes of age

The Court's Authority over Guardian and Ward.

Even where the father has the custody and care of his own children, such children may, nevertheless, be considered wards of Court In cases of this kind the Court exercises jurisdiction over the father exactly as it would over a guardian,[3] and although it would be necessary to bring forward strong proof, yet the Court will in a proper case remove the children out of the control of their father. It is only when the injury to a child is clearly proved that the Court will interfere in such cases [4]

---

[1] 36 and 37 Vict, Ch 12   [2] See p 60
[3] *In re Plumley*, 45 L T R, 283
[4] *Shelley v Westbrooke*, 23 R R 47, and see p 55 as to Guardianship of Infants Act, 1886, Sec 7 As to other cases where the parents are deprived of the control of children, see pp 27 *et seq*

A ward of Court may not marry without the consent of the Court. If this rule is broken, all the parties concerned are guilty of contempt of Court and may be punished by imprisonment until the contempt is purged This rule applies even although the parents are living and give their consent to the marriage Where an application is made to the Court by any person desiring to marry a ward of Court, the matter is referred to Chambers, an enquiry is made as to the suitability of the match, and the question of a settlement is raised. The ward cannot be compelled to make a settlement, although the Court generally directs the other party to enter into a settlement. If the marriage has already taken place without the Court's consent, the settlement will be drawn in accordance with the wishes of the Court, and although a ward cannot be compelled to agree to such settlement, yet the other party, where the ward is a female, may be imprisoned until a settlement is arrived at [1]

Maintenance.

A father is under a legal duty to provide food, clothing, shelter, and education for his infant children If such infant children have property in their own right, such fact does not give the father the right to any payment out of such property for the maintenance of the infant children [2] He remains at common law bound to support them As, however, the Court always leans towards making such provision for children as would fit them for the enjoyment of their future fortune, an allowance may be made even to the parents for the maintenance of the children,[3] but not as of right [4]

The guardian, other than the parents, will receive such allowance for the child's maintenance as is suitable to the child's expectations ; that is, such an amount as will be sufficient to maintain and educate the child in the station of life in which the amount of his fortune is likely to cause him to be placed Where such an allowance is made, the amount allowed should be expended for the purpose for which it is allowed, as no profit should be made by the guardian out of his guardianship Thus, where the child was in the care of its mother, and certain funds were placed at her disposal for the maintenance of

---

[1] *Field* v *Moore*, 7 De G M and G 691
[2] But see Conveyancing Act, 1881, 44 and 45 Vict , Ch 41, Sec 43, p 59
[3] *Havelock* v *Havelock*, 17 Ch Div 807
[4] *Meacher* v *Young*, 2 My and K 490

the child, it was held that where she had not expended the funds on the child's maintenance, she was liable to account [1]

Although the question of maintenance of infants entitled in the future to property will touch only a small percentage of children, yet it may not be out of place to notice what provision has been made for the maintenance of infants entitled to property by virtue of a deed containing no express trust for maintenance.

Conveyancing Act, 1881.

The Conveyancing and Law of Property Act, 1881,[2] enacts that—

"Where any property is held by trustees in trust for an infant, either for life, or for any greater interest, and whether absolutely, or contingently on his attaining the age of twenty-one years, or on the occurrence of any event before his attaining that age, the trustees may, at their sole discretion, pay to the infant's parent or guardian, if any, or otherwise apply for or towards the infant's maintenance, education, or benefit, the income of that property, or any part thereof, whether there is any other fund applicable to the same purpose, or any person bound by law to provide for the infant's maintenance or education, or not"

Provision is made for investment and accumulation of surplus income and for the application of such accumulations to the above purposes if necessary. The provisions of this section apply in all cases in which the trust deed does not exclude the operation of the section.

These provisions make the necessity of application to the Court in an average case unusual

The Conveyancing Act, 1881,[3] also provides for the management of an infant owner's real estate, giving to the trustees ample powers for the administration of the estate and power to pay out of income at their discretion sums for the maintenance, education, or benefit of the infant either themselves applying such sums for such purposes or paying them to the infant's parent or guardian

Further detail on the above matters would be out of place in this volume, but the reader is referred to the Statute itself and to standard works on Equity and Real Property

---

[1] *Macrae v Harness*, 103 L.T R 629
[2] 44 and 45 Vict, Ch 41, Sec 43   [3] Sec 42

CHAPTER V

RELIGIOUS EDUCATION

BLACKSTONE, in his *Commentaries*,[1] says—

"The last duty of parents to their children is that of giving them an education suitable to their situation in life ; a duty pointed out by reason and of far the greatest importance of any For as Puffendorf very well observes[2] ' it is not easy to imagine or allow that a parent has conferred any considerable benefit upon his child by bringing him into the world, if he afterwards entirely neglects his culture and education, and suffers him to grow up like a mere beast, to lead a life useless to others and shameful to himself' Yet the municipal laws of most countries seem to be defective on this point by not constraining the parent to bestow proper education upon his children Perhaps they thought it punishment enough to leave the parent who neglects the instruction of his family to labour under those griefs and inconveniences which his family so uninstructed will be sure to bring upon him Our laws, though their defects in this particular cannot be denied, have in one instance made a wise provision for breeding up the rising generation , since the poor and laborious part of the community when past the age of nurture are taken out of the hands of their parents by the statutes for apprenticing poor children ,[3] and are placed out by the public in such a manner as may render their abilities in their several stations of the greatest advantage to the commonwealth The rich, indeed, are left at their option whether they will breed up their children to be ornaments or disgraces to their family"

At common law the rights of the father are absolute as against all the world, and in one respect he has, except in extreme cases, the absolute right of controlling the religious education of his child ; the common law, therefore, lays down no limit or standard of education except such as fits the child for his station in life, a very vague and indecisive standard, as education was thought of little moment, and a minimum would formerly fit a person for any station

---

[1] Book I, p 450
[2] *Law of Nations*, Book VI, Ch 2, p 12
[3] 5 Eliz , Ch 4 , 43 Eliz , Ch 2 , 1 Jac I , Ch 25 , 7 Jac I , Ch 3 , 8 and 9 Wm & M , Ch 30 , 2 and 3 Anne, Ch 6 , 4 and 5 Anne, Ch 19 , 17 Geo II, Ch. 5 , 18 Geo III , Ch 47.

in life It is only in modern times that steps have been taken to cast upon parents the duty of educating their children, and in England in particular the question of education has been intimately mixed with matters of religion. Before dealing with the purely secular side of education, it may be well to notice briefly the attitude of the law towards the father's rights in relation to religious education

A father cannot, by any agreement, ante-nuptial or post-nuptial, repudiate his right to control the religious education of his children ; the right that he has to such control is not given to him for his own benefit but for that of his children [1] That this was so may be gathered from Blackstone's statement as to the limits placed upon a person's absolute right to control the religious education of his children ; he says, in relation to the parent's duty to educate his children—

"Yet in one case, that of religion, they are under peculiar restrictions ; for it is provided [2] that if any person sends any child under his government beyond the seas, either to prevent its good education in England or in order to enter into or reside in any popish college or to be instructed, persuaded, or strengthened in the popish religion, in such cases, besides the disabilities so incurred by the child so sent, the parent or person sending shall forfeit £100 which shall go to the sole use and benefit of him that shall discover the offence , and if any parent or other shall send or convey any person beyond the sea to enter into or be resident in, or to be trained up in any priory, abbey, nunnery, popish university, college, or school, or a house of jesuits or priests, or in any private popish family, in order to be instructed, persuaded, or confirmed in the popish religion, or shall contribute anything towards their maintenance when abroad by any pretext whatever, the person both sending and sent shall be disabled to sue in law or equity or be executor or administrator to any person or to enjoy any legacy, or deed of gift, or to bear any office in the realm and shall forfeit all his goods and chattels and likewise all his real estate for life." [3]

Other evidence that the child's benefit was the primary consideration so far as political and religious intolerance would allow was that a Roman Catholic parent was forbidden to refuse a

---

[1] *In re Agar-Ellis* v *Lascelles*, 10 Chancery Division, 49.
[2] 1 Jac I, Ch 4, and 3 Jac I, Ch 5
[3] 3 Car I, Ch 2, and Blackstone's *Commentaries*, Book I, p 451

fitting maintenance to his Protestant child with a view to compel him to change his religion, and that this law was extended to the case of Jewish parents who were bound to provide for their Protestant children maintenance suitable to the fortune of the parent and the age and education of the child.[1] To-day the father has full and free choice in his religion, but at the same time his rights must be exercised for the children's benefit. In *Agar-Ellis* v. *Lascelles*[2] the facts before the Court were that a Protestant father on his marriage with a Roman Catholic wife, had undertaken that all the children should be brought up as Roman Catholics. After the marriage he determined that they should follow his religion, but the mother, without his knowledge, instructed the children until at last they refused to go to a Protestant church. The father made them wards of Court and the Court granted an injunction to restrain the mother from taking them to any other than a Protestant place of worship. Where, however, the father has abdicated his parental right to control the children's religious education and the ages of the children are such that the grant of a renewal of such rights would be injurious to the children's welfare, the Court will not interfere.[3] The maxim which usually applies in this case is *Religio sequitur patrem*, and, except in special circumstances, even after the death of the father, the children must be brought up in the religious faith of the father or according to his wishes.[4] Even where the authority of the Court is invoked for the protection of a child either from parental cruelty or neglect, or where a child shows criminal tendencies, or where a child is made a ward of Court, the religion of the father is the basis upon which the child's religious education is built up. Thus the various Acts relating to the prevention of cruelty to children have provided that, in determining the person to have the custody of a child who is taken under an order made by the Court for the protection of such child, the Court must endeavour to select one of the same religious persuasion as the child, or one who gives an undertaking that the child shall be brought up in its own religion.[5] The Education Acts, 1870-1912, have carefully preserved the rights of parents in relation to the control of religious education.

---

[1] 11 and 12 Wm III, Ch 4 ; 1 Anne, Statute I, Ch 30
[2] 10 Ch Div 49   [3] *Re Newton* (1896), 1 Chancery, 740
[4] *Re Scanlan*, 40 Ch Div, 200.   [5] See Children Act, 1908, Sec 23, p 30

The Elementary Education Act, 1870[1] makes the following provision—

"Every elementary school which is conducted in accordance with the following regulations shall be a public elementary school within the meaning of this Act, and every public elementary school shall be conducted in accordance with the following regulations (a copy of which regulations shall be conspicuously put up in every such school), namely—

"(1) It shall not be required as a condition of any child being admitted into or continuing in the school that he shall attend or abstain from attending any Sunday school or place of religious worship or that he shall attend any religious observances or any instruction in religious subjects in the school or elsewhere from which observance or instruction he may be withdrawn by his parents, or that he shall, if withdrawn by his parent, attend the school on any day exclusively set apart for religious observance by the religious body to which his parent belongs [2]

"(2) The time or times during which any religious observance is practised, or instruction in religious subjects is given at any meeting of the school shall be either at the beginning or at the end or at the beginning and the end of such meeting, and shall be inserted in a time-table to be approved by the education department[3] and to be kept permanently and conspicuously affixed in every schoolroom, and any scholar may be withdrawn by its parent from such observance or instruction without forfeiting any of the other benefits of the school

"(3) The school shall be open at all times to the inspection of any of His Majesty's Inspectors so, however, that it shall be no part of the duty of such inspector to inquire into any instruction in religious subjects given at such school or to examine any scholar therein in religious knowledge or in any religious subject or book"

Even in the case of children who have been wards of Court, the authority of the father and the control of the child's religious education by the father will not be interfered with except where the father has forfeited his rights by gross immorality, or where by his conduct he has abdicated his parental control [4] The custody and education of infants so far at any rate as religion is concerned, is in the hands of the Chancery Division, and the Judicature Act, 1873, provides that the rules of equity are for the future to prevail in all Courts equally, and therefore in interpreting any provision as to

---

[1] Sec 7
[2] *e g*, Ascension Day, *Marshall* v *Graham*, 97 L T R 52, see p 65
[3] Now Board of Education.   [4] *Shelley* v *Westbrook*, 23 R R 47

education, the Courts, if asked to interfere with a parent's right would have regard to that course which would be of the greatest benefit to the infant.

An illegitimate child being *nullius filius* in the eye of the law cannot have any legal guardian; but the mother has obligations imposed upon her, and in return has vested in her certain parental rights[1] including the control of the child and of its education.

[1] *Barnardo v McHugh*, 1891, A C. 388.

CHAPTER VI

SECULAR EDUCATION

THE first definite attempt to place an efficient elementary secular education within reach of all classes by means of legislation was the Elementary Education Act, 1870.[1] This Act, which provided for the erection of school boards,[2] gave power to such school boards to make by-laws in respect of the education of children in their respective areas. Section 74 of the Act is to the following effect—

Section 74.—Every school board may from time to time, with the approval of the education department,[3] make by-laws for all or any of the following purposes—

(1) Requiring the parents of children of such age, not less than five nor more than thirteen[4] years as may be fixed by the by-laws, to cause such children (unless there is some reasonable excuse) to attend school.

(2) Determining the time during which children are so to attend school, provided that no such by-law shall prevent the withdrawal of any child from any religious observance or instruction in religious subjects, or shall require any child to attend school on any day exclusively set apart[5] for religious observance by the religious body to which his parent belongs, or shall be contrary to anything contained in any Act for regulating the education of children employed in labour.[6]

(3) Providing for the remission of payment of the whole or any part of the fees of any child where the parent satisfies the school-board that he is unable from poverty to pay the sum.

(4) Imposing penalties for the breach of any by-laws.

(5) Revoking or altering any by-law previously made. Provided that any by-law made under this section requiring a child between ten[7] and thirteen years of age to attend school shall provide for the total or partial exemption of such child from obligation to attend school if one of Her Majesty's Inspectors certifies that such child has reached a standard of education specified in such by-laws.

---

[1] 33 and 34 Vict., Ch. 75
[2] Abolished by 2 Ed. VII, Ch. 42
[3] Now Board of Education
[4] Now "fourteen," Sec. 6 (1), Elem. Ed. Act, 1900
[5] e.g., Ascension Day, *Marshall* v *Graham*, 97 L.T.R. 52
[6] *Mellor* v *Denham*, 4 Q.B.D. 241, also 43 and 44 Vict., Ch. 23, Sec. 4
[7] Now "eleven," 56 and 57 Vict., Ch. 42, Sec. 1

Any of the following reasons[1] shall be a reasonable excuse for non-attendance, namely—

(1) That the child is under efficient instruction in some other manner;

(2) That the child has been prevented from attending school by sickness or any unavoidable cause;

(3) That there is no public elementary school open which the child can attend within such distance, not exceeding three miles measured according to the nearest road from the residence of such child, as the by-laws may prescribe.[2]

It has on several occasions[3] been laid down that the specified grounds set out in section 74 of the Education Act, 1870, are not the only grounds of excuse open to a parent when information is laid against him for not causing his child to attend school. It has recently been laid down that a child, if a member of the Church of England, may be withdrawn from school on Ascension Day, as that day is a "day exclusively set apart for religious observance"[4] by the Church of England. Hence it will be a reasonable excuse for non-attendance on certain days that the child was withdrawn on such days as being days exclusively set apart by the Church for religious observance.

Section 7, sub-section 1, of the Elementary Education Act, 1870,[5] provides—

"It shall not be required as a condition of any child being admitted into, or continuing in, the school that he shall attend or abstain from attending any Sunday school or place of religious worship, or that he shall attend any religious observance or any instruction in religious subjects in the school or elsewhere from which observance or instruction he may be withdrawn by his parent, or *that he shall attend the school on any day exclusively set apart for religious observance by the religious body to which his parents belong.*"

It was suggested that this provision was made for the benefit of Jews and Roman Catholics, but Lord Alverstone[6] refused to

---

[1] And others, *Isle of Wight County Council* v *Holland* (1909), 101 L T R. 861, also *Rex* v. *W Riding Justices* (1910) 2 K B 192

[2] No longer available as excuse if means of conveyance provided, Sec 14, 7 Ed VII, Ch 43

[3] *Marshall* v *Graham*, and *Bell* v *Graham*, 97 L T R 52

[4] Secs 7 and 14, Elem Ed Act, 1870

[5] 33 and 34 Vict, Ch 75

[6] *Marshall* v *Graham*, 97 L.T R 52, per Lord Alverstone, C J at p 57

accept this view. The provision of section 74 (2) like that in section 7 is intended for the benefit of all parents and of all religions Section 74 allows by-laws to be made provided—

"That no such by-law shall prevent the withdrawal of any child from any religious observance or instruction in religious subjects, or shall require any child to attend school on any day exclusively set apart for religious observance by the religious body to which his parent belongs."

The school board,[1] not less than one month before submitting any by-law under section 74 for approval of the education department,[2] shall deposit a copy of the proposed by-law at their office for inspection by any ratepayer, and supply a printed copy thereof gratis to any ratepayer, and shall publish a notice of such deposit

The education department[2] before approving any by-laws shall be satisfied that these conditions as to deposit, publication, and supply of printed copies when required have been complied with and shall hold such inquiry in the district as they think requisite. By-laws come into force when sanctioned by the Board of Education.

The by-laws when sanctioned can be enforced summarily and penalties recovered, but with costs the penalty must not exceed 20s[3] for each offence.

Model by-laws[4] have been framed for the guidance of local authorities. These by-laws fix the ages of children to attend school at "not less than five nor more than fourteen" They provide that the time of attendance shall be the whole time for which the school selected shall be open for inspection No provision is made for the remission of fees. If this model is followed, approval of the Board of Education is almost certain, but any material deviation would probably not be sanctioned.

Where the local education authority is a county council, the power to make by-laws includes a power to make different by-laws for different parts of the area controlled by the authority[5] This is necessary, as the conditions in a rural and an urban area in the same county may be very different.

[1] Now Local Education Authority
[2] "Board of Education," Elem Ed Act, 1900, Sec 6 (3)
[3] Elem Ed Act, 1900, 63 and 64 Vict, Ch 53, Sec 6 (2)
[4] P 78, infra
[5] Education Act, 1902, 2 Ed VII, Ch. 42, Sec 3 (4)

Attendance Order.

Provision is made as to legal proceedings in the Elementary Education Act, 1873 [1] By this Act justices may, instead of inflicting a penalty, make an order that the child shall attend school according to the by-laws, and if the order is not complied with the parent or person against whom it is made is liable to a penalty not exceeding the penalty to which he is liable for failure to comply with the by-law [2]

Presumption of Age.

Where a child is apparently within the ages covered by the by-laws and so liable to attend school, the onus of proving that the child is not of such age is on the person charged with failing to cause the child to attend school.[3] Further, the onus is on the defendant to show that the school the child attends, if other than a public elementary school, is efficient, and the test of efficiency is based on the age of the child and the requirements of the Board of Education as to the standard of education for a child of such age.[4]

The Education Act, 1876,[5] goes much further than the Act of 1870 It creates a statutory duty[6] that a parent shall cause his children between five and fourteen[7] to receive efficient elementary instruction in reading, writing, and arithmetic, and lays down rules for the enforcement of such statutory duty quite apart from the by-laws which are made by a local authority under section 74 of the principal Act.[8]

First laying down the limits within which children may be taken into employment, it then proceeds to set out the machinery to prevent employment during school age and consequent absence from school [9]

It is on the construction of section 74 of the Education Act, 1870, and of sections 11 and 12 of the amending Act of 1876 that a large amount of litigation has taken place Several cases relating

---

[1] 36 and 37 Vict, Ch 86, Secs. 23 to 25
[2] Sec. 24 (3) See p. 97 [3] Sec 24, ss 6
[4] Sec 24, ss. 7. [5] 39 and 40 Vict, Ch 79
[6] *Infra L C C* v. *Hearn* (1909), 78 L J, K B. 414
[7] 39 and 40 Vict, Ch 79, Sec 48
[8] 33 and 34 Vict., Ch. 75, Sec. 74.
[9] See Employment.

to the construction of by-laws and of these sections have come before the Courts recently and the facts of these will be set out after stating the provisions of section 11.[1]

11. If either—

"(1) the parent of any child above five years who is under this Act prohibited[2] from being taken into full time employment habitually and without reasonable excuse neglects to provide efficient elementary instruction for his child; or

Attendance Order.

"(2) any child is found habitually wandering or not under proper control, or in the company of rogues, vagabonds, disorderly persons, or reputed criminals, it shall be the duty of the local authority after due warning of the parent of such child, to complain to a Court of summary jurisdiction, and such Court if satisfied with the truth of the complaint shall order that the child do attend some certified efficient school[3] willing to receive him, and named in the order, being either such as the parent may select, or if he do not select any, then such public elementary school as the Court think expedient, and the child shall attend that school every time that school is open,[4] or in such other regular manner as is specified in the order."

An order under this section is referred to as an *attendance order*

Excuses for Non-attendance.

Any of the following reasons shall be a reasonable excuse—

(1) That there is not within two miles,[5] measured according to the nearest road from the residence of such child, any public elementary school open which the child can attend; or

(2) That the absence of the child from school has been caused by sickness or any unavoidable cause.

These reasons are not the only reasons open to a parent as reasonable excuses;[6] among others it is sufficient if the parent shows that his child is receiving *efficient* instruction at home.[7] What is, in general, a reasonable excuse for non-compliance with by-laws

---

[1] 39 and 40 Vict, Ch 79
[2] Sec 5, and see *Winyard v Toogood* (1882), 10 Q.B D 218
[3] Sec 48
[4] Compare model by-laws under Sec 74, Act, 1870, p 78
[5] By-laws limit three miles. Not now an excuse if a conveyance is provided under the power given to local authorities by 7 Ed VII, Ch 43, Sec 14
[6] See *infra*, p 71
[7] *Rex v West Riding Justices* (1910), 2 K B 192.

under the Act of 1870 is a reasonable excuse for non-compliance with an order under section 11 of the Act of 1876

Before 1880 it was doubtful whether proceedings could be taken in all cases under section 11 above cited, or under by-laws at the local authority's option. When, on application to a magistrate by a school board for a summons against a parent of a child for not causing it to attend school, contrary to by-laws made by the Board under the Elementary Education Act, 1870,[1] it appeared that the parent had *habitually neglected* to provide instruction within the meaning of the Elementary Education Act, 1876,[2] it was held to be the duty of the magistrate to refuse the summons, the proper procedure being to take out a summons under section 11, for the option given by section 50 of the Act of proceedings under the statute or under the by-laws applies only to offences punishable under the Act, and the offence of habitual neglect is not so punishable.[3] This is set at rest by section 4 of the Elementary Education Act, 1880,[4] which provides that—

"Proceedings may in the discretion of the local authority or person instituting the same, be taken for punishing the contravention of a by-law, notwithstanding that the act or neglect or default alleged as such contravention constitutes habitual neglect to provide efficient elementary education for a child within the meaning of section 11 of the Elementary Education Act, 1876."

The following cases are a few of those decided during recent years on points of construction under the Act and under by-laws.

An education authority under its powers under section 74 of the Elementary Education Act, 1870,[5] as amended by the Education Acts, 1876 to 1902, made School Attendance By-laws which were sanctioned by the Board of Education on 16th February, 1904 These by-laws provided (*inter alia*) that—

"The parent of every child of not less than five and not more than fourteen years of age shall cause such child to attend school unless there be a reasonable excuse for non-attendance"

Any of the following shall be a reasonable excuse, namely—

(a) That the child is under efficient instruction in some other manner,

---

[1] 33 and 34 Vict, Ch 75, Sec 74   [2] 39 and 40 Vict, Ch 79, Sec 11.
[3] *London School Board* v *Bridge*, *In re* Murphy (1872) 2 Q B D 397
[4] 43 and 44 Vict, Ch 23.   [5] 33 and 34 Vict, Ch. 75

(b) That the child has been prevented by sickness or other unavoidable cause;

(c) That there is no public elementary school within three miles, in the case of a child over seven years of age, and one mile in the case of a child under seven years of age, measured according to the nearest road from the residence of such child

Proviso

"A child between thirteen and fourteen years of age shown to the satisfaction of the local authority *to be beneficially employed* shall not be required to attend school if such child has obtained a certificate that it has made 350 attendances after five years of age in not more than two schools during each year for five years whether consecutive or not."

In *Holloway (app.) v Crow (Resp.)*[1] where the construction of the by-laws was called in question, it was held that under the by-laws the onus of proof that a child was beneficially employed was on the parent, that whether the child was beneficially employed or not was a question for the local education authority and not for the justices, that reasonable excuse for the child's non-attendance would not be limited to the particular reasonable excuses provided in the by-laws[2] It was further held that the justices would not be entitled to say that nursing was a reasonable excuse generally although they might say so on a particular occasion, their opinion depending on the facts of the case

Non-compliance with an Attendance Order.

When a parent is summoned under section 12 of the Act of 1876 for non-compliance with an order made under section 11, he is not confined to the two excuses specified as reasonable in section 11, but he is entitled to any reasonable excuse for non-compliance

Reasonable Excuses.

In *Rex v. Morris and others, Justices of the West Riding, Ex parte Broadbent*,[3] it was held that a parent upon whom an attendance

---

[1] (1911) 1 K B 636, and 105 L T R 73
[2] *Rex v Morris and others, West Riding Justices* (1910), 2 K B 192
[3] 102 L T R 814 (1910), 2 K B 192 See also *Belper School Attendance Committee v Bailey*, 9 Q B D 259, *Hewitt v. Thompson*, 60 L.T.R.; *London School Board v. Duggan*, 13 Q.B.D. 176.

order is served is entitled to give evidence that he is giving the child in respect of whom the order is made an efficient elementary instruction at home, and if he proves that he is giving such efficient instruction it is a reasonable excuse for non-compliance with the order, inasmuch as " the reasonable excuse within the meaning of the Act" in section 12 is not restricted to the two reasonable excuses mentioned in the Act in section 11.

Part Attendance Elsewhere.

In *Isle of Wight County Council (app.)* v. *Holland (resp.)*[1] the respondent was summoned under section 12 of the Elementary Education Act, 1876,[2] for failing to comply with an attendance order by which his child was required to attend a certain school. Since the date of the order the child had been withdrawn from the school named in the order and entered as a pupil at another public elementary school under the same local authority The child had only attended twenty-nine times out of a total possible forty-six times during which the school had been open in five weeks. It was held that such irregular attendance at another school was not sufficient excuse for non-compliance with the order as the child was not attending the other school so as to constitute a reasonable excuse within section 12 of the Act.

Truancy.

In *Hewitt* v. *Thompson*[3] the parent of the child on whom an attendance order had been served under section 11 of the Elementary Education Act, 1876, gave as an excuse that he had used every endeavour, short of taking the child to the school door, to ensure its attendance, but that failure to attend was due to the child's truancy It was held that this was no reasonable " excuse " within the meaning of the Act, and that the magistrate had therefore jurisdiction to order the child to be sent to an industrial school

Although this case has been overruled in that it is now no authority for saying that the " reasonable excuse " must be one of those enumerated in the by-laws under the Elementary Education

---

[1] *Isle of Wight County Council* (app) v *Holland* (resp), 101 L T R 861
[2] 39 and 40 Vict, Ch. 79.   [3] 53 J.P. 103, 60 L T. 268.

Act, 1870, section 74, or in section 11 of the Act of 1876,[1] it has been affirmed on the point above cited.[2]

The rule that it is not a reasonable excuse that a child has failed to attend school by its own fault and not owing to its parents' neglect has recently been confirmed, and under such circumstances the magistrate may make an attendance order under section 11 of the Elementary Education Act, 1876.[3] Proof of the fact of non-attendance without any reasonable excuse is sufficient grounds for the making of the order.[4]

Efficient Elementary Education.

Mere attendance at a private school will not be sufficient excuse for non-compliance with an attendance order if the magistrates, as a fact, are satisfied that a child, in respect of whom such order is made, is not receiving *efficient* elementary education at such private school.[5]

In an appeal to the Divisional Court of the King's Bench the following facts came to light. The appellant was summoned for neglecting to provide *efficient* elementary instruction for a child. Evidence was given that the child was attending a private school where there was only one room which adjoined a factory and that the general equipment was inefficient. It was also proved that the instruction given to the child in the school was inefficient. The magistrate found that the appellant had habitually and without reasonable excuse neglected to provide efficient elementary instruction, and he made an order that the child should attend a certain elementary school in the district.

It was contended that evidence as to the building was wrongly admitted, but Lord Alverstone said—[6]

" Even assuming that certain topics were introduced which were irrelevant, the magistrate knew that the appellant was summoned for neglecting to find *efficient* elementary instruction for the child, and in my opinion he has applied his mind to that point. He has stated as a fact that the child was not being provided with

---

[1] *Rex* v *West Riding Justices* Ex parte Broadbent (1910), 2 K.B. 192 102 L T R 81
[2] *London C   Council* v *Hearn*, 100 L T R 438, 73 J P 211
[3] 39 and 40   t , Ch 79
[4] *London (ty Council* v. *Hearn*, 100 L.T R 438
[5] *Shiers* v   *enson*, 105 L T R 522   [6] At p 523

efficient elementary instruction at the school in question. We cannot say that the magistrate has gone wrong in law, and, therefore, the appeal must be dismissed."

Private Tuition.

On the other hand, attendance at a private school or tuition by a private teacher may be efficient instruction of the kind required by the Act. Whether it is or is not is a question of fact In *Bevan* (app.) v. *Shears* (resp.)[1] this question was discussed By the by-law of the local education authority under the Education Act, 1870,[2] and its amending Acts 1876 to 1902 " the parent of every child of not less than five years nor more than fourteen years of age shall cause such child to attend school unless there be a reasonable excuse for non-attendance" "That the child is under efficient instruction in some other manner" was *inter alia* a reasonable excuse.

Efficient Instruction in a Private School.

The respondent had placed his child with a private teacher, and on information against the respondent for contravening the above by-law, the justices held that the instruction received from the private teacher was efficient It was held that the justices rightly dismissed the information and that it was competent for them to decide that the education was efficient without determining that the instruction of the private teacher was as efficient as the child would have received in a public elementary school. Mr. Justice Darling in his judgment said—

" If we agree with the appellant's contention we should have to say that if the child had been educated at a good State school in Germany according to the curriculum of that country, he would not be receiving efficient instruction, and that parents must be convicted because the instruction that the child was receiving in Germany did not compare with the curriculum of the . . . . . . School The fact that the German curriculum differed from that of an English elementary school might be the reason for the parent sending his child to Germany The same observation might be made if the child had been sent to Eton or to a French lycée."[3]

[1] (1911), 2 K B 936, and 105 L T R 795.
[2] Sec 74. [3] 105 L.T R at p 796.

Exclusion, Reasonable Excuse.

Saunders v *Richardson*,[1] already referred to, is an authority which decides that attendance must be *effective attendance* in order that the requirements of the by-law under section 74 of the Elementary Education Act, 1870, may be complied with. It was clearly laid down that merely sending a child to the school with a certainty that it would be sent away was not sufficient, and that such sending away was not a *reasonable excuse* for non-attendance.

Non-payment of Fees.

In this case a child was sent to the school where fees were charged and payable in advance. The parent was able to pay but refused to give the fees to the child and in consequence the child was refused admission. The father was, nevertheless, liable to be convicted on account of the child's non-attendance.

Again, where a parent persisted in sending his child to the wrong school at which admission was properly refused, it was held that the parent had no excuse for the child's non-attendance.[2]

Verminous Children.

The most recent case on the question of exclusion of children from school as an excuse for non-attendance is *Walker* (app.) v *Cummings* (resp.)[3] In this case the parent of the child which was not exempt from compulsory attendance at school sent the child to school in such a verminous condition that the child was refused admission to the school and it had been refused admission on previous occasions for similar reasons. Its condition was capable of remedy by means within reach of the parent and might have been easily cured. Upon information against the parent for not "causing his child to attend school," the justices were of the opinion that the parent had used some means but not the best to cleanse the child, and that its condition could have been cured, but they were also of opinion that the condition of the child would not have prevented it from receiving instruction, and they held that the refusal to admit the child was a "reasonable excuse" for non-attendance and they dismissed the information. The

---

[1] 7 Q B D. 388. [2] *Jones* v *Rowland*, 80 L.T R 630
[3] (1912) 107 L T R 304

Divisional Court, however, held that the parent having knowingly sent the child to school in such a condition that admission would be refused[1] had not "caused the child to attend school" within the meaning of the by-laws applicable, and that he had no "reasonable excuse" and ought to have been convicted.

Code Article 53b.

Counsel for the appellant drew the attention of the Court to Article 53*b* of the Education Code which provides that the condition in which the child was is a reasonable ground for refusing to admit a child to the school. Quite apart from the Education Code the legislature has made special provision for the removal of verminous children from school.

8 Ed. VII, Ch. 67, Section 122.

The Children Act, 1908, in section 122 makes the following provision—

"A local education authority may direct their medical officer, or any person provided with, and if required, exhibiting the authority in writing of their medical officer to examine in any public elementary school provided or maintained by the authority, the person and clothing of any child attending the school, and if on examination the medical officer or any such authorised person as aforesaid is of opinion that the person or clothing of any such child is infected with vermin or is in a foul or filthy condition, the local education authority may give notice in writing to the parent or guardian or any person liable to maintain the child, requiring him to cleanse properly the person and clothing of the child within twenty-four hours after the receipt of the notice"

Right to Remove and Cleanse.

If the person to whom any such notice is given fails to comply within such twenty-four hours, the medical officer or some other person provided with, and if required exhibiting, the authority in writing of the medical officer may remove the child referred to in the notice from any such school and may cause the person and clothing of the child to be properly cleansed in suitable premises and with suitable appliances, and may, if necessary for that purpose, without

---

[1] *Saunders v Richardson*, 7 Q B.D 388.

any warrant other than the provision of the Act,[1] convey to such premises and there detain the child until the cleansing is effected.

Means of Cleansing.

Where any sanitary authority within the district of a local education authority have provided, or are entitled to the use of, any premises or appliances for cleansing the person or clothing of persons infested with vermin, the sanitary authority shall, if so required by the local education authority, allow the local education authority to use such premises and appliances for the above purpose upon such payment (if any) as may be agreed between them or in default of agreement settled by the Local Government Board.

Repeated Uncleanliness.

Where, after the person or clothing of a child has been cleansed by a local education authority under this section, the parent or guardian of or other person liable to maintain the child allows him to get into such a condition that it is again necessary to proceed under this section, the parent, guardian, or other person shall, on summary conviction, be liable to a fine not exceeding 10s.

Instructions to Parents.

Where a local education authority gives notice under section 122 of the Children Act to the parent or guardian of, or other person liable to maintain the child, requiring him to cleanse the person and clothing of the child, the authority shall also furnish him with written instructions describing the manner in which the cleansing may best be effected

The examination and cleansing of girls under this section shall only be effected by a duly qualified medical practitioner or by a woman duly authorised in writing by the medical officer.

In *Walker* v *Cummings*[2] it was evident that proceedings had been taken under the authority of this section, and it was, therefore, quite unnecessary for counsel to rely upon the Education Code, Article 53b, although that Article was equally applicable If the headmaster, however, without any written authority from

---

[1] Children Act, Sec 122 [2] 107 L T.R. 304, *supra.*

the medical officer, excludes a child from school on account of its condition he will do so in reliance on the Education Code.

Obligation to make By-laws.

It is now the *duty* of the local education authority of every school district to make by-laws under section 74 of the Elementary Education Act, 1870.[1] Where the local education authority fails, the Board of Education may make by-laws which shall have effect and be enforced as if they had been made by the local authority. The following is the form of by-laws issued to school boards (and now applying to local education authorities under the Act of 1902) by the Board of Education—

FORM OF BY-LAWS ISSUED TO SCHOOL BOARDS BY THE BOARD OF EDUCATION

By-laws made under section 74 of the Elementary Education Act, 1870, as amended by the Education Acts, 1876, 1880, 1899, 1900.

For the (District)
For the (Local Authority).

DEFINITION

(i)—In these by-laws—

The term "district" means (name of district)

The term "child" means a child residing in the district.

The term 'school" means a certified efficient school

"Attendance" means an attendance at a morning or afternoon meeting of the school

The code "for the time being" means a code of minutes of the Board of Education in force for the time being in respect to the Parliamentary grant to public elementary schools in England

The term "local authority" means a local authority for the district acting for the time being under the Elementary Education Act, 1876 [2]

CHILDREN TO ATTEND SCHOOL

(ii).—The parent of every child of not less than five nor more than fourteen years of age shall cause the child to attend school unless there is a reasonable excuse[3] for non-attendance

The following reasons[4] shall be reasonable excuses, namely—

(*a*) That the child is under efficient instruction in some other manner ;

---

[1] Elem Ed Act, 1880, 43 and 44 Vict, Ch 23, Sec 2.
[2] And amending Acts
[3] *Rex* v. *Morris and others* (1910), 2 K B. 192   [4] And others.

(*b*) That the child has been prevented from attending school by sickness or any unavoidable cause ;

(*c*) That there is no public elementary school open which the child can attend within (*number of miles not more than three*) miles, measured according to the nearest road from the residence of such child.

TIME OF ATTENDANCE

(iii).—The time during which every child shall attend school shall be the whole time for which the school selected shall be open for the instruction of children of similar age including the day fixed by His Majesty's Inspector for his annual visit.

PROVISO AS TO RELIGION AND LABOUR ACTS

(iv).—Provided always that nothing in these by-laws—

(*a*) shall prevent the withdrawal of any child from any religious observance of instruction in religious subjects ;

(*b*) shall require any child to attend school on any day exclusively set apart[1] for religious observance by the religious body to which its parent belongs ; or

(*c*) shall have any force or effect in so far as it may be contrary to anything contained in any Act for regulating the education of children employed in labour.

PROVISO AS TO PARTIAL EXEMPTION

(v).—And provided always that—

(*a*) a child between twelve and fourteen years of age being beneficially employed to the satisfaction of the local authority has either—

(1) received a certificate from one of His Majesty's Inspectors of Schools that he has reached the (*necessary standard not lower than the 4th, but lower than the standard in the proviso for total exemption*) standard prescribed by the code for the time being, or

(2) obtained a certificate that it has made 300 attendances in not more than two schools in each year for five preceding years whether consecutive or not,

such child may—

(*x*) while regularly making five attendances in each week in which the school is open, be exempt from further attendance at school, or may—

(*y*) after having completed 200[2] attendances during a period

---

[1] *Marshall* v. *Graham*, 97 L T R 52.
[2] Any number not less than 200.

from[1] _____ to[2] _____ subsequent thereto be exempt from further attendance until[3] _____next ensuing

Special by-law for children to be employed in Agriculture (under 62 & 63 Victoria, Chapter 13)

(b) the parent of any child may at any time if such child is eleven years of age and has passed the fifth[4] standard, give notice to the local authority that such child is to be employed in agriculture

The minimum age for total exemption from school attendance for such child shall be thirteen.

Such child while between the ages of eleven and thirteen shall attend school 250 times in the year, namely—(state period or periods within which attendance must be made)

Any such child as soon as it has made the number of attendances required for the period or periods above mentioned shall, whilst employed in agriculture be exempt from further obligation to attend school until the_____[5]

The certificate from the head teacher of a school that such child has made the attendances required by this by-law together with the production of the labour certificate shall be sufficient evidence to justify the employment in agriculture of such child

PENALTY

(vi) —Every parent who shall not observe or shall neglect or violate these by-laws or any of them shall, upon conviction, be liable to a penalty not exceeding with costs twenty shillings for each offence

REVOCATION

(vii) —Any by-laws heretofore made under section 74 of the Elementary Education Act, 1870, or under that section as amended by the Elementary Education Acts, 1876, 1880, 1893, 1899, 1900, are hereby revoked as from the day on which the present by-laws shall come into operation

The above by-laws were made by the X local authority at a meeting held on the_____day of_____19__

In witness whereof the school board[6] have hereunto set their common seal this_____day of_____19____

Sealed in the presence of_____Chairman
_____Clerk

[1] and [2] Limits of the period during which partially exempted children are to be in attendance

[3] The last date to which the exemption extends or the commencement of the next period of attendance

[4] Or some higher standard

[5] End of the year or next succeeding period above mentioned

[6] Now Education Authority.

It may be noted that by-laws which have received the sanction of the Board of Education are not invalid merely because they may contain more stringent provisions than those contained in the Act of 1876. Further particulars as to school attendance are contained in a later chapter on the Employment of Children

Certain classes of children have, during the last decade, been specially provided for Thus it is now no excuse that a child is suffering from physical or mental defects rendering it undesirable that his education be continued with that of children suffering from no such defects The next chapter sets out the present provisions of the law in this respect

CHAPTER VII

THE EDUCATION OF CHILDREN SUFFERING FROM PHYSICAL AND MENTAL DEFECTS

THE provisions of the Elementary Education Act, 1876, that a parent must cause his child to receive efficient elementary instruction in reading, writing, and arithmetic are in relation to a blind or deaf child construed to mean efficient instruction having regard to the child's peculiar circumstances [1] The fact that a child is blind or deaf is not a reasonable excuse for neglecting to provide efficient elementary instruction for the child after, in the case of a deaf child, that child has reached the age of seven.

Definitions of "Blind and Deaf" Child.

The expression "blind child" means "a child too blind to read the ordinary school books used by children," and the expression "deaf child" means "a child too deaf to be taught in a class of hearing children in an elementary school"

Definition of "Child"

The usual age limits for education do not apply to deaf and blind children, but for purposes of education they are deemed to be children until they reach the age of sixteen years, and the period of compulsory education extends to this age, and no such child may take advantage of the by-laws of an education authority as to total or partial exemption from the obligation to attend school. [2]

It is the duty of every local education authority towards all blind and deaf children resident in their district, for whom efficient and suitable elementary education has not otherwise been provided, to obtain such education for such child in a school certified by the Board of Education as suitable for that purpose The education authority may, for this purpose, either establish or maintain, or contribute towards the expenses of, a school to such extent as may be approved by the Board of Education and make arrangements

---

[1] Elem Ed (Blind and Deaf Children) Act, 1893, 56 and 57 Vict, Ch 42, Sec 1
[2] 56 and 57 Vict, Ch 42, Sec 11

subject to the regulations of the Board of Education for boarding out any blind or deaf child in a home conveniently near a certified school.[1]

Religious Instruction.

In selecting a school for any deaf or blind child, the school authority shall have regard to the religious persuasion of the child's parent, and the child shall not be compelled to receive religious instruction contrary to the wishes of the parent, and facilities shall, as far as practicable, be provided for the child to receive religious instruction in accordance with the parent's persuasion.

Parent's Contribution towards Expense.

Where the local education authority incur any expense in respect of a blind or deaf child, the parent of the child shall be liable to contribute towards the expenses of the child, such weekly sum as may be agreed between the school authority and the parent, or, if the parties fail to agree, as may be settled by a Court of summary jurisdiction, the sum so agreed or settled being recoverable from the parent as a civil debt.

Who is Parent?

The term "parent" often includes other persons than the natural parent, and a recent decision has been come to on the interpretation of this word. The word "parent" is defined in the Act to include every person who is liable to maintain the child.

The question of liability of guardians to contribute under this description was discussed in *Guardians of the Southwark Union* (apps.) v. *London County Council* (resp.)[2] Although the guardians are liable to maintain a pauper child it was held that the guardians are not persons liable to maintain under the definition of parent and so not the "parent" within section 9 (1) of the Act in question.[3] They cannot, therefore, be called upon to contribute to the expenses of a local authority which has undertaken the duty of providing for a deaf orphan child under section 2 of the Act, even although such child would be destitute if turned out of school and thus would become immediately chargeable to the guardians

---

[1] Sec. 2 [2] 102 L T R 747. [3] 56 and 57 Vict., Ch. 42.

The Board of Education may assist a certified school by a grant in respect of the education of blind or deaf children

Defective Children.

No provision was made for the case of defective and epileptic children apart from the general provisions as to education until 1899 when the Elementary Education (Defective and Epileptic Children) Act[1] was passed. Under this Act and the amending Act of 1914,[2] a local education authority must ascertain and make such arrangements as they think fit for ascertaining what children in their district, not being imbecile nor merely dull and backward, are defective, i.e., by reason of mental or physical defect are incapable of taking advantage and benefiting from the instruction in ordinary elementary schools and are not capable by reason of such defect of receiving benefit in special schools provided for them. Similar inquiries must be made as to what children, not being idiots or imbeciles, are unfit by reason of severe epilepsy to attend the ordinary public elementary schools.[3] The Act of 1914 creates a duty to adopt the earlier Act. Advantage has been taken of the Acts in most of the larger educational areas. The London County Council, besides their medical officers, employ a psychologist for the special purpose of studying cases brought to his notice by headmasters of schools. A great difficulty under the Acts is the objection of parents to any inquiry into the mental condition of their children being made, but this is overcome by the compulsion of the Acts. If, on the other hand, a parent is of the opinion that a child ought to be dealt with under the Acts, the local education authority are to provide facilities for enabling any parent to present such child to be examined. Failure on the part of the authority to do so is a contravention of the Acts. The term "parent" as used in this connection includes the guardian and every person who is liable to maintain or who has the actual custody of the child.[4]

If a child is defective or epileptic, a certificate to that effect by a duly qualified practitioner approved by the Board of Education is required after an examination conducted in the presence of

---

[1] 62 and 63 Vict, Ch 32 [2] 4 & 5 Geo V, ch 45
[3] 62 and 63 Vict, Ch 32, Sec 1
[4] 33 and 34 Vict, Ch 75, Sec 3, and 56 and 57 Vict, Ch 42, Sec 15, but see *Guardians of the Southwark Union* v L C C, 102 L T R 747

the parent of such child It is the duty of the parent to attend such examination, and failure to do so when notified by the local education authority is punishable by fine, on summary conviction, not exceeding £5. The causes which render an epileptic child unfit to attend an ordinary school are that serious disturbance to the work of the school may be caused or that the child is a serious danger to itself. Where it has been ascertained that there are defective children whose respective ages exceed seven years within the area administered by a local authority, provision must be made for their education either in public elementary schools where special classes are maintained or in certified special schools near which children may be boarded out, or in more populous areas by the establishment of schools for defective children A local education authority have the same power of contributing to or maintaining schools on terms approved by the Board of Education for defective and epileptic children as they have in the case of blind and deaf children [1] Examinations are to be conducted from time to time of children dealt with under the provisions of the Acts for the purpose of ascertaining whether or not the mental and physical condition of any child has so improved as to fit him for attendance at an ordinary elementary school Failure to make such periodical examinations is a contravention of the Acts

Guides or conveyances may be provided for children who are unable by reason of physical or mental defects to attend school without such assistance [2] In the opinion of the Board of Education this provision is not limited to children attending special classes, but may be taken advantage of to meet the case of children who would, by reason of *physical* defect, be incapable of attending an ordinary elementary school [3]

As in the case of blind and deaf children the duty of a parent to provide elementary instruction for his child shall, in the case of a defective or epileptic child over seven years of age, where a school having certified special classes or a special school is within reach of the child's residence, include the duty to cause the child to attend such classes or school, and it is not a reasonable excuse that the authority have not provided a guide or conveyance

[1] 62 & 63 Vict, Ch. 32, Sec 2   [2] Sec 3
[3] See also 7 Ed VII, Ch 43, Sec 14 as to general power to provide conveyances

A local education authority may apply to a Court of summary jurisdiction for an order requiring a child to be sent to a certified school for epileptics, and if the parent fails to comply with the order he may be proceeded against as if he had failed to comply with an attendance order under the Elementary Education Act, 1876.[1] The parent of a defective or epileptic child is liable to contribute towards the expenses of the child incurred by the local education authority, but will not be thereby deprived of any franchise or subject to any disability.[2]

"Child."

The period during which a defective or epileptic boy or girl is deemed to be a child is up to the age of sixteen years, and compulsory attendance at school, therefore, extends to this age and may be enforced as if it were required by the by-laws of the local education authority, but under no such by-law is such a child entitled to partial or total exemption.[3]

Bodily Health in Relation to Education.

Just as in the matter of protection of children the tendency is towards the promotion of mental and moral well-being, so in education as a corollary the aim is to promote physical well-being

Meals for School Children.

Modern legislation has been directed towards the making of a sound body as a first step towards training a sound mind. All educationalists are agreed that under-fed, badly-clothed, and ill-tended children cannot take that advantage of educational facilities which the cost of provision requires As a step in the right direction the Education (Provision of Meals) Act, 1906,[4] was passed extending the powers given to a local education authority as established by Part III of the Education Act, 1902 [5]

6 Ed. VII, Ch. 57.

A local education authority may take such steps as they think fit for the provision of meals for children in attendance at any public elementary school in their area, and for that purpose—

(a) may associate with themselves any committee on which

---

[1] Sec 4, but see 4 & 5 Geo 5, Ch 45, Sec. 4 (2).   [2] Sec. 8
[3] Sec 11   [4] 6 Ed. VII, Ch. 57   [5] 2 Ed VII, Ch 42

the authority are represented, who will undertake to provide food for those children (in the Act called a "school canteen committee"); and

(b) may aid that committee by furnishing such land, buildings, furniture, apparatus, and such officers and servants as may be necessary for the organisation, preparation, and service of such meals.

The authority may only incur expense in respect of purchasing food under certain circumstances set out in section 3 of the Act.

Authority's Right to Defray Expense of Food.

Where the local education authority resolve that any of the children attending an elementary school within their area are unable by reason of lack of food to take full advantage of the education provided for them, and have ascertained that funds other than public funds are not available or are insufficient in amount to defray the cost of food furnished in meals under the Act, they may apply to the Board of Education, and that Board may authorise them to spend out of the rates such sum as will meet the cost of provision of such food

The amount to be expended in this manner must not exceed the amount which would be produced by a halfpenny rate over the area of the authority in any financial year. If the authority is a county council other than the London County Council, the area in question is the parish or parishes which the school serves

Parent's Liability.

The local education authority must charge the cost of each meal furnished under the Act to the parent of the child. If the parent fails to pay, the authority may recover the amount as a civil debt, but such failure will not, as in the case of Poor Law relief, cause the parent any loss of franchise or subject him to disability. If the parent is unable to pay from circumstances other than his own fault, the authority are not obliged to require the payment

It should be noted that there was formerly no power to provide meals for children during vacation, but the law is now amended by the Education (Provision of Meals) Act, 1914[1] under which Act the powers of a local authority in this matter may be exercised both

---

[1] 4 & 5 Geo V, c 20

on days when the school meets and on other days. This seems a useful provision in this time of distress, but it has been urged that the ties of family and the responsibilities of parents tend to be loosened and the duty to provide food, clothing, and lodging for the children they bring into the world, the primary duty of man, is only too likely to be neglected and left to the care of the nation

Medical Treatment Cost.

By the Local Education Authorities (Medical Treatment) Act, 1909,[1] it is provided that where any local education authority provides for the medical treatment of children attending any public elementary school under section 13 of the Education (Administrative Provisions) Act, 1907,[2] there shall be charged to the parent of every child in respect of any treatment provided for that child such amount not exceeding the cost of treatment as may be determined by the local education authority, and in the event of payment not being made by the parent it shall be the duty of the authority, unless they are satisfied that the parent is unable by reason of circumstances other than his own default to pay the amount, to require the payment of that amount from the parent. Any sum so charged to a parent may be recovered summarily as a civil debt, but failure to pay does not entail the consequences that acceptance of Poor Law relief would in relation to the franchise, nor does it cause the parent any disability

Cost of Education.

The charge for education is a local one, each authority being responsible for the cost of educating children in their area. It sometimes happens that a child lives on the border between two districts under the control of separate education authorities. In these circumstances parents often wish to choose a school under one authority while actually residing in the area of the other authority Under these circumstances one local education authority will be educating the children of another at the expense of the former's ratepayers

It is now provided that contributions may be claimed in respect

---

[1] 9 Ed VII, Ch 13   [2] 7 Ed VII, Ch 43

of such children [1] The provision of the legislature on this point is as follows—

" Where any children resident in the area of any local education authority [2] . . . are receiving education in any public elementary school within the area of some other local education authority, the Board of Education may, if they think fit, on the application of that other local education authority (in this section referred to as the applicant authority) and after giving the first-named local education authority (in this section referred to as the respondent authority) an opportunity of being heard, make a contribution order under this section."

A contribution order means an authority directing the respondent authority to pay to the applicant authority annually such sum as the Board think proper in respect of children resident in the area of the respondent authority who, in the opinion of the Board, are properly receiving education in a public elementary school within the area of the applicant authority

The Board of Education shall have regard to the interests of secular instruction, to the wishes of parents as to the education of their children, and to economy of rates, before making an order under the Act

[1] Education (Admin Prov) Act, 1911, 1 and 2 Geo V, Ch 32
[2] 2 Ed VII, Ch 42, Sec 1

CHAPTER VIII

EDUCATION AND THE PREVENTION AND PUNISHMENT OF CRIME

The care and education of children who by reason of being youthful criminals or of being left in circumstances in which special treatment is necessary is provided for in the Children Act, Part IV, which has replaced after repeal all the Acts relating to reformatory and industrial schools

The expression "reformatory school" means a school for the industrial training of youthful offenders, in which youthful offenders are lodged, clothed, and fed, as well as taught. The expression "industrial school" means a school for the industrial training of children in which children are lodged, clothed, and fed, as well as taught Such schools require to be "certified schools," which expression means a reformatory or industrial school which is certified in accordance with the provisions[1] of Part IV of the Act.

Definition of the word "Child" for Part IV.

The expression "child" used in reference to a child ordered to be sent to a certified industrial school or to be transferred from a certified reformatory to a certified industrial school applies to that child during the whole period of detention, whether in the industrial school or out on licence, notwithstanding that the child attains the age of 14 years before the expiration of that period, and, when used in reference to proceedings for the purpose of enforcing an attendance order, includes any person who, by virtue of any enactment, is deemed to be a child for the purposes of the Education Act, 1870 to 1907

The persons for the time being having the management or control of a school shall be deemed the managers thereof [2]

Certification and Inspection of Certified Schools.

The Secretary of State may, upon the application of the managers of any reformatory or industrial school, direct the chief inspector

---
[1] Sec. 45.   [2] Sec. 44, Ed VII, Ch 67.

of reformatory and industrial schools hereinafter mentioned to examine into the condition and regulations of the school and its fitness for the reception of youthful offenders or children to be sent there under Part IV of the Children Act, and to report to him thereon.

The Secretary of State, if satisfied with the report of the inspector, may certify that the school is fit for the reception of such youthful offenders or children [1]

Every certified school shall at least once in every year be inspected by the chief inspector of reformatory and industrial schools, or by an inspector or assistant inspector appointed by the Secretary of State [2]

Power to Withdraw Certificate.

The Secretary of State, if dissatisfied with the condition, rules, management, or superintendence of a certified school, may at any time by notice served on the managers of the school declare that the certificate of the school is withdrawn as from a time specified in the notice, being not less than six months after the date of the notice; and at that time the withdrawal of the certificate shall take effect, and the school shall cease to be a certified school

The Secretary of State may, however, if he thinks fit, instead of withdrawing the certificate, by notice served on the managers of the school prohibit the admission of youthful offenders or children to the school for such time as may be specified in the notice or until the notice is revoked [3]

Resignation of Certificate.

The managers of a certified school may, on giving six months', and the executors or administrators of a deceased manager (if only one) of a certified school may, on giving one month's notice in writing to the Secretary of State of their intention to do so, resign the certificate for the school, and accordingly, at the expiration of the six months or one month (as the case may be) from the date of the notice (unless before that time the notice is withdrawn), the resignation of the certificate shall take effect, and the school shall cease to be a certified school [4]

[1] Sec 45
[2] Sec 46.
[3] Sec 47.
[4] Sec. 48

Effect of Withdrawal or Resignation of Certificate.

A youthful offender or child shall not be received into a certified school after the date of the receipt by the managers of the school of a notice of withdrawal of the certificate for the school or after the date of a notice of resignation of the certificate; but the obligation of the managers to teach, train, lodge, clothe, and feed any youthful offenders or children detained in the school at the date of any notice given or received shall, except so far as the Secretary of State otherwise directs, continue until the withdrawal or resignation of the certificate takes effect, or until the discontinuance of the contribution out of money provided by Parliament towards the expenses of the offenders and children detained in the school, whichever may first happen.[1]

Disposal of Inmates on Withdrawal or Resignation of Certificate.

Where a school ceases to be a certified school, the youthful offenders or children detained therein shall be by order of the Secretary of State either discharged or transferred to some other certified school.[2]

Auxiliary Homes.

Where the managers of a certified school, or the managers of two or more certified reformatory schools or of two or more certified industrial schools, propose to establish an auxiliary home for the reception of any inmates or any classes of inmates of the school or schools, or to utilise for any such purpose an institution already in existence or about to be established by any other persons, the Secretary of State may, on an application and report such as is required in the case of the schools themselves, certify the home or institution. Such certificate may be withdrawn and resigned in like manner as a certificate of a school, but whilst the home or institution remains certified it shall for such purposes as are specified in the certificate be treated as part of the school or schools to which it is attached.[3]

Liabilities of Managers.

The managers of a certified school may decline to receive any youthful offender or child proposed to be sent to them, but when

[1] Sec. 49.   [2] Sec. 50.   [3] Sec. 51.

once they have accepted any such offender or child they are deemed to have undertaken to train, teach, lodge, clothe, and feed him during the whole period for which he is liable to be detained in the school, or until the withdrawal or resignation of the certificate for the school, or until the discontinuance of the contribution provided by Parliament towards the expenses of the offenders or children detained in the school, whichever may first happen.[1]

Boarding Out of Children.

The managers of a certified industrial school to which a child under the age of eight years is sent may, with the consent of the Secretary of State, board the child out with any suitable person until the child reaches the age of ten years and thereafter for such longer period, with the consent of the Secretary of State, as the managers consider to be advisable in the interests of the child, subject to the exercise by the managers of such powers as to supervision, recall, and otherwise as may be prescribed by regulations made by the Secretary of State; and where a child is so boarded out he shall, nevertheless, be deemed to be a child detained in the school, and the provisions of Part IV of the Children Act shall apply accordingly, subject to such necessary adaptations as may be made by Order in Council.[2]

Power to Make Rules.

The managers of a certified school may at any time, and shall, whenever so required by the Secretary of State, make rules for the management and discipline of the school, subject to approval by the Secretary of State.[3]

SENDING OFFENDERS AND CHILDREN TO REFORMATORY AND INDUSTRIAL SCHOOLS

Commitment of Offenders between twelve and sixteen Years of Age to Reformatory Schools.

Where a youthful offender, who in the opinion of the Court before which he is charged, is twelve years of age or upwards but less than sixteen years of age, is convicted, whether on indictment or by a petty sessional Court, of an offence punishable in the case of an adult with penal servitude or imprisonment, the Court may, in

[1] Sec 52   [2] Sec 53   [3] Sec 54

addition to or in lieu of sentencing him according to the law to any other punishment, order that he be sent to a certified *reformatory* school. Where, however, the offender is ordered to be sent to a certified reformatory school he shall not, in addition, be sentenced to imprisonment.

Where such an order has been made in respect to a youthful offender of the age of fourteen years or upwards, and no certified reformatory school can be found the managers of which are willing to receive him, the Secretary of State may order the offender to be brought before the Court which made the order or any Court having the like jurisdiction, and that Court may, in lieu of the detention order, make such order or pass such sentence as the Court may determine, so, however, that the order or sentence shall be such as might have been originally made or passed in respect of the offence.[1]

Power to send Offenders Conditionally Pardoned to Reformatory Schools.

Where a youthful offender[2] has been sentenced to imprisonment or penal servitude, and has been pardoned by His Majesty on condition of his placing himself under the care of some charitable institution for the reception and reformation of youthful offenders, the Secretary of State may direct him, if under the age of sixteen years, to be sent to a certified reformatory school, the managers of which consent to receive him, for a period of not less than three and not more than five years, but not in any case extending beyond the time when he will in the opinion of the Secretary of State attain the age of nineteen years; and thereupon the offender shall be subject to all the provisions as if he had been originally sentenced to detention in a certified reformatory school.[3]

Children Liable to be sent to Industrial Schools.

Any person may bring before a petty sessional Court any person apparently under the age of fourteen years who—

(a) is found begging or receiving alms (whether or not there is any pretence of singing, playing, performing, offering anything for sale, or otherwise), or being in any street, premises, or place for the purpose of so begging or receiving alms; or

[1] Sec. 57
[2] Compare " youthful delinquents," 4 & 5 Geo. V, Ch. 58, Sec. 10
[3] Sec. 84

(b) is found wandering and not having any home or settled place of abode, or visible means of subsistence, or is found wandering and having no parent or guardian, or having a parent or guardian who does not exercise proper guardianship ; or

(c) is found destitute, not being an orphan and having both parents or his surviving parent, or in the case of an illegitimate child his mother, undergoing penal servitude or imprisonment ; or

(d) is under the care of a parent or guardian who, by reason of criminal or drunken habits, is unfit to have the care of the child ; or

(e) is the daughter whether legitimate or illegitimate of a father who has been convicted of an offence under section 4 or section 5 of the Criminal Law Amendment Act, 1885,[1] in respect of any of his daughters, whether legitimate or illegitimate ; or

(f) frequents the company of any reputed thief, or of any common or reputed prostitute, or

(g) is lodging or residing in a house or the part of a house used by any prostitute for the purposes of prostitution or is otherwise living in circumstances calculated to cause, encourage, or favour the seduction or prostitution of the child ;

and the Court before which a child is brought as coming within one of those descriptions, if satisfied on inquiry of that fact, and that it is expedient so to deal with him, may order him to be sent to a certified industrial school. Provided that a child shall not be treated as coming within the description contained in paragraph (f) if the only common or reputed prostitute whose company the child frequents is the mother of the child, and she exercises proper guardianship and due care to protect the child from contamination.

It shall be the duty of the police authority to take proceedings as respects any child in their district who appears to the authority to come within one of the descriptions mentioned, unless—

(a) the case is one within the cognisance of the local education authority and that authority decide themselves to take proceedings, or

(b) proceedings are being taken by some other person ; or

(c) the police authority are satisfied that the taking of proceedings is undesirable in the interests of the child

[1] 48 and 49 Vict, Ch 69

It may be noticed here that a child sent to an industrial school, unlike one sent to a reformatory, is not necessarily a youthful offender, but where a child apparently under the age of twelve years is charged before a Court of assize or quarter sessions or a petty sessional Court with an offence punishable in the case of an adult by penal servitude or a less punishment, the Court, if satisfied on inquiry that it is expedient so to deal with the child, may order him to be sent to a certified industrial school

First Offences.

Where a child, apparently of the age of twelve or thirteen years, who has not previously been convicted, is charged before a petty sessional Court with an offence punishable in the case of an adult by penal servitude or a less punishment, and the Court is satisfied that the child should be sent to a certified school but, having regard to the special circumstances of the case, should not be sent to a certified reformatory school, and is also satisfied that the character and antecedents of the child are such that he will not exercise an evil influence over the other children in a certified industrial school, the Court may order the child to be sent to a certified industrial school, having previously ascertained that the managers are willing to receive the child. The Secretary of State may, on the application of the managers of the industrial school, by order transfer, where necessary, such child to a certified reformatory school.[1]

Child Out of Control.

Where the parent or guardian of a child proves to a petty sessional Court that he is unable to control the child, and that he desires the child to be sent to an industrial school, the Court, if satisfied on inquiry that it is expedient so to deal with the child, and that the parent or guardian understands the results which will follow may order him to be sent to a certified industrial school If the Court thinks that it is expedient that the child, instead of being sent to a certified industrial school, should be placed under the supervision of a probation officer, the Court may deal with him in like manner as if he had been charged with an offence for which the Court might have dealt with him under the Probation of Offenders Act, 1907,[2] so, however, that the recognisance on entering

---
[1] Sec 58
[2] 7 Ed VII, Ch 17, amended by 4 & 5 Geo V, Ch 58, Sec 7

into which he is discharged shall bind him to appear for having a detention order made against him.

Refractory Children in Workhouse.

Where the guardians of a poor law union or the managers of a district poor law school satisfy a petty sessional Court that any child maintained in a workhouse or district poor law school is refractory, or is the child of parents either of whom has been convicted of an offence punishable with penal servitude or imprisonment, and that it is desirable that the child be sent to an industrial school, the Court may, if satisfied that it is expedient so to deal with the child, order him to be sent to a certified industrial school

Education Authority's Complaint.

A petty sessional Court may, on the complaint of a local education authority, made in accordance with the provisions of section 12 of the Elementary Education Act, 1876, for the purpose of enforcing an attendance order, order a child to be sent to a certified industrial school as provided in that section [1] If upon such complaint it appears to the Court that the child comes within one of the descriptions mentioned in sub-section 1 [2] of section 58, the Court may, on the application of the local education authority, proceed under that sub-section and not under section 12 of the Elementary Education Act, 1876

Where, under this section, a Court is empowered to order a child to be sent to a certified industrial school, the Court, in lieu of ordering him to be so sent, may, in accordance with the provisions of Part II of the Children Act,[3] make an order for the committal of the child to the care of a relative or other fit person named by the Court

Power to Commit Young Persons to Care of Relative or Fit Person in Certain Cases.

Any person may bring before a petty sessional Court any person apparently of the age of fourteen or fifteen years so circumstanced that if he were a child he would come within one or other of the descriptions rendering him liable to be sent to an industrial school,

---

[1] As to defective children see 4 & 5 Geo V, Ch 45, Sec 4 (2)
[2] See *supra*, p 94   [3] Under Sec 21

and the Court, if satisfied on inquiry of that fact and that it is expedient so to deal with him, may, in accordance with the provisions of Part II of the Children Act, make an order for his committal to the care of a relative or other fit person named by the Court.[1]

Young Persons Under Supervision of Probation Officer.

Where, under this power, an order is made for the committal of a child or young person to the care of a relative or other fit person named by the Court, the Court may, in addition to such order, make an order under the Probation of Offenders Act, 1907,[2] that the child or young person be placed under the supervision of a probation officer. See also Criminal Justice Administration Act, 1914 [3]

Provided that the recognisance into which the child, if not charged with an offence, or the young person is required to enter shall bind him to appear and to submit to the further order of the Court [4]

Power to Defer Operation of Order.

A "detention order" of a Court ordering a youthful offender or child to be sent to and detained in a certified school may, if the Court thinks fit, be made to take effect either immediately or at any later date specified therein, regard being had to the age or health of the youthful offender or child [5]

Choice of School.

The school to which a youthful offender or child is to be sent under a detention order shall be such school as may be specified in the order, being some certified school (whether situate within the jurisdiction of the Court making the order or not) the managers of which are willing to receive the youthful offender or child. If, however, it is found impossible to specify the school in the detention order, the school shall, subject to the place of residence of a youthful offender or child, be such as a justice having jurisdiction in the place where the Court which made the order sat may by indorsement on the detention order direct. Special provision is made for defective children to receive special training in special schools [6]

---

[1] Sec 59   [2] 7 Ed VII, Ch 17   [3] 4 & 5 Geo V, Ch 58, Secs 7-9
[4] Sec. 60.   [5] Sec 61   [6] Sec 62

Temporary Detention Until Sent to Certified School.

If—

(a) a detention order is made but is not to take effect immediately ; or

(b) at the time specified for the order to take effect the youthful offender or child is unfit to be sent to a certified school, or

(c) the school to which the youthful offender or child is to be sent cannot be ascertained until inquiry has been made,

the Court may make an order committing him either to custody in any place [1] to which he might be committed on remand, or to the custody of a relative or other fit person to whose care he might be committed under Part II of the Children Act, [2] and he shall be kept in that custody until he is sent to a certified school in pursuance of the detention order [3]

Conveyance to School.

The person by whom any youthful offender or child ordered to be sent to a certified school is detained shall, at the appointed time, deliver him into the custody of the constable or other person responsible for his conveyance to school, who shall deliver him to the superintendent or other person in charge of the school in which he is to be detained, together with the detention order or other document in pursuance of which the offender or child was detained and is sent to school. The detention order shall be a sufficient authority for his conveyance to and detention in the school or in any other school to which he is transferred [4]

Period of detention.

The detention order shall specify the time for which the youthful offender or child is to be detained in the school, being—

(a) in the case of a youthful offender sent to a reformatory school, not less than three and not more than five years, but not in any case extending beyond the time when the youthful offender will, in the opinion of the Court, attain the age of nineteen years, and

(b) in the case of a child sent to an industrial school such time as the Court may deem proper for the teaching and training of the child, but not in any case extending beyond the time

---

[1] Sec. 108. [2] Sec. 21. [3] Sec. 63. [4] Sec. 64

when the child will, in the opinion of the Court, attain the age of sixteen years [1]

Provision as to Religious Persuasion.

The Court or justice in choosing the school to which a youthful offender or child is to be sent, shall endeavour to ascertain the religious persuasion to which the offender or child belongs, and the detention order shall, where practicable, specify the religious persuasion to which the offender or child appears to belong, and a school conducted in accordance with that persuasion shall, where practicable, be selected [2]

A minister of the religious persuasion specified in the order as that to which a youthful offender or child sent to a certified school appears to belong may visit the offender or child at the school on such days, at such times, and on such conditions as may be fixed by the Secretary of State, for the purpose of affording him religious assistance and also for the purpose of instructing him in the principles of his religion

Where an order has been made for sending a youthful offender or child to a certified school which is not conducted in accordance with the religious persuasion to which the offender belongs, the parent, legal guardian, nearest adult relative, or person entitled to the custody of the offender or child may apply to remove or send the offender or child to a certified school conducted in accordance with the offender's or child's religious persuasion If the detention order was made by a petty sessional Court, the application is made to a petty sessional Court acting in and for the place in and for which the Court which made the order acted ; and in any other case to the Secretary of State The Court or Secretary of State shall, on proof of the offender's or child's religious persuasion, comply with the request of the applicant

The application must be made before the offender or child has been sent to a certified school, or within thirty days after his arrival at the school ; and the applicant must show to the satisfaction of the Court or Secretary of State that the managers of the school named by him are willing to receive the offender or child [3]

---

[1] Sec 65
[3] Sec 66
[2] See religious education, *supra*, p 60

Placing Out on Licence.

Where a youthful offender or child is detained in a certified school, the managers of the school may at any time by licence, permit the offender or child to live with any trustworthy and respectable person named in the licence willing to receive and take charge of him

The consent in the case of a child sent to an industrial school at the instance of the local education authority, of that authority, and in any other case of the Secretary of State is required for the granting of such licence After the expiration of eighteen months of the period of detention no such consent is needed

Where the licence, which is revokable at any time, is granted in respect of a child under fourteen years, it shall be conditional on the child attending as a day scholar, in accordance with the by-laws in force in the place where he resides, some school named in the licence, being a certified efficient school within the meaning of the Elementary Education Act, 1876 [1] Any licence so granted shall be in force until revoked or forfeited by the breach of any of the conditions on which it was granted

Escape Whilst on Licence.

Any youthful offender or child escaping from the person with whom he is placed in pursuance of this section, or refusing to return to school when required to do so on the revocation or forfeiture of his licence, shall be liable to the same penalty as if he had escaped from the school itself.

The time during which a youthful offender or child is absent from a certified school in pursuance of a licence under this section, shall be deemed to be part of the time of his detention in the school But where a youthful offender or child has failed to return to the school on the licence being forfeited or revoked, the time which elapses after his failure so to return shall be excluded in computing the time during which he is to be detained in the school

Where a licence has been revoked or forfeited and the youthful offender or child refuses or fails to return to the school, a Court of summary jurisdiction, if satisfied by information on oath that there is reasonable ground for believing that his parent or guardian could produce the youthful offender or child, may issue a summons

---

[1] 39 and 40 Vict., Ch 79,

requiring the parent or guardian to attend at the Court on such days as may be specified in the summons, and to produce the child, and, if he fails to do so without reasonable excuse, he shall, in addition to any other liability to which he may be subject,[1] be liable on summary conviction to a fine not exceeding £1.[2]

Supervision After the Expiration of Period of Detention.

Every youthful offender sent to a certified reformatory school shall, on the expiration of the period of his detention, if that period expires before he attains the age of nineteen years, remain up to the age of nineteen years under the supervision of the managers of the school.

Every child sent to an industrial school shall, from the expiration of the period of his detention, remain up to the age of eighteen under the supervision of the managers of the school. Where, however, the child was ordered to be sent to an industrial school for the purpose only of enforcing an attendance order made in consequence of his parent, guardian, or other person legally liable to maintain him neglecting to provide efficient elementary instruction for him, the supervision of managers does not continue

Parents' Powers Limited.

When a youthful offender or child is under the supervision of the managers of a certified school, it shall not be lawful for his parent to exercise, as respects the youthful offender or child, his rights and powers as parent in such a manner as to interfere with the control of the managers over the youthful offender or child.

The managers may grant to any person under their supervision a licence as already described and may revoke any such licence, and recall any such person to the school; and any person so recalled may be detained in the school for a period not exceeding three months, and may at any time be again placed out on licence. But a person shall not be so recalled unless the managers are of opinion that the recall is necessary for his protection, and the managers shall send to the chief inspector of reformatory and industrial schools an immediate notification of the recall of any person, and shall state the reasons for his recall; and they shall again place the person out as soon as possible, and at latest within

[1] Sec. 72.   [2] Sec. 67.

three months after the recall, and shall forthwith notify the chief inspector that the person has been placed out.

A licence granted to a youthful offender or child before the expiration of his period of detention shall, if he is liable to be under supervision in accordance with this section, continue in force after the expiration of that period, and may be revoked in the manner above mentioned

The Secretary of State may at any time order that a person under supervision shall cease to be under such supervision.[1]

Discharge and Transfer.

The Secretary of State may at any time order a youthful offender or a child to be discharged from a certified school, either absolutely or on such conditions as the Secretary of State approves, and may, where the order of discharge is conditional, revoke the order on the breach of any of the conditions on which it was granted, and thereupon the youthful offender or child shall return to school, and if he fails to do so, he and any person who knowingly harbours or conceals him or prevents him from returning to school shall be liable to the same penalty as if the youthful offender or child had escaped from the school

The Secretary of State may order—

(a) a youthful offender or child to be transferred from one certified reformatory school to another, or from one certified industrial school to another ;

(b) a youthful offender under the age of fourteen years detained in a certified reformatory school to be transferred to a certified industrial school ;

(c) a child over the age of twelve years detained in a certified industrial school, who is found to be exercising an evil influence over the other children in the school to be transferred to a certified reformatory school ;

so, however, that the whole period of the detention of the offender or child shall not be increased by the transfer [2]

Where a youthful offender or child is detained in a certified school in one part of the United Kingdom, the " central authority " (i e, the Secretary of State, the Secretary for Scotland, or the Chief Secretary, as the case may be) for that part of the United Kingdom

---

[1] Sec. 68.   [2] Sec. 69

may direct the youthful offender or child to be transferred to a certified school in another part of the United Kingdom if the "central authority" for that other part consents [1]

Power to Apprentice or Dispose of Child.

If any youthful offender or child detained in or placed out on licence from a certified school, or a person when under the supervision of the managers of such a school conducts himself well, the managers of the school may, with his own consent, apprentice him to, or dispose of him in, any trade, calling, or service, including service in the Navy or Army, or by emigration, notwithstanding his period of detention or supervision has not yet expired; and such apprenticing or disposition shall be as valid as if the managers were his parents But where he is disposed of by emigration, and in any case unless he has been detained for twelve months, the consent of the Secretary of State shall also be required for the exercise of any power under this section [2]

OFFENCES IN RELATION TO CERTIFIED SCHOOLS

If a youthful offender detained in a certified reformatory school is guilty of a serious and wilful breach of the rules of the school, or of inciting other inmates of the school to such a breach, he shall be liable upon summary conviction to have the period of his detention in the reformatory school increased by such period not exceeding six months as the Court directs, or if of the age of sixteen years or upwards, to be imprisoned, with or without hard labour, for any term not exceeding three months; and if sentenced to imprisonment he shall, at the expiration of the term thereof, by and at the expense of the managers of the school in which the offence was committed, be brought back to a certified reformatory school, there to be detained during a period equal to so much of his period of detention as remained unexpired at the time of his being sent to prison

If a child of the age of twelve years or upwards detained in a certified industrial school is guilty of a serious and wilful breach of the rules of the school or of inciting other inmates of the school to such a breach, he shall be liable on summary conviction to be sent to a certified reformatory school, and to be there detained, subject

---

[1] Sec 69, ss 3.   [2] Sec. 70

and according to the provisions relating to detention in reformatory schools

A period of detention may be increased in pursuance of this section, notwithstanding that the period as so increased will extend beyond the limits imposed by the Children Act.

Escaping from School.

If a youthful offender detained in a certified reformatory school escapes from the school, he may, at any time before the expiration of his period of detention, be apprehended without warrant, and may (any other Act to the contrary notwithstanding) be then brought before a Court of summary jurisdiction having jurisdiction in the county or place where he is found, or in the county or place where the school from which he escaped is situate, and he shall be liable on summary conviction to be brought back to the reformatory school and to have the period of his detention therein increased by such period not exceeding six months as the Court directs, or, if of the age of sixteen years or upwards, to be imprisoned with or without hard labour, for any term not exceeding three months; and if sentenced to imprisonment he shall, at the expiration of the term thereof, be brought back to a certified reformatory school

If a child detained in a certified industrial school escapes from the school, he may at any time before the expiration of his period of detention be apprehended without warrant, and may (any other Act to the contrary notwithstanding) be then brought before a Court of summary jurisdiction having jurisdiction in the county or place where he is found, or in the county or place where the school from which he is escaped is situate, and he shall be liable on summary conviction to be brought back to the school from which he escaped, or, if of the age of twelve years or upwards, to be sent to a certified reformatory school

In computing the time during which a youthful offender or child who, having escaped, is brought back to a certified school is thereafter liable to be detained in that school, the time during which he was absent from school including the time (if any) during which he was imprisoned under this section, shall not be reckoned as part of the period of detention

Where the period for which a youthful offender or child, on being brought back to the school from which he escaped, is liable to be detained therein would, by virtue of this section, whether on account of any increase in the period of detention or otherwise, extend beyond the limits imposed by Part IV of the Children Act,[1] the youthful offender or child may, notwithstanding, be detained in the school in accordance with the above rules.[2]

Assisting Person Escaped from such School.

If any person—

(a) knowingly assists or induces directly or indirectly an offender or child detained in or placed out on licence from a certified school to escape from the school or from any person with whom he is placed out on licence;

(b) or knowingly harbours, conceals, or prevents from returning to school, or to any person with whom he is placed out on licence, an offender or child who has so escaped, or knowingly assists in so doing;

he shall on summary conviction be liable to be imprisoned for any term not exceeding two months, with or without hard labour, or to a fine not exceeding £20.

The expenses of bringing a youthful offender or child back to the school shall be borne by the managers of the school from which he escaped.

Every officer authorised by the managers of a certified school or by a local education authority to take charge of any youthful offender or child ordered to be detained under this Part of this Act for the purpose of conveying him to or from the school, or of apprehending and bringing him back to the school in case of his escape or refusal to return, shall, for that purpose and while engaged in that duty, have all the powers, protection, and privileges of a constable.[3]

Expenses of Certified Schools.—Contributions from Treasury.

Money provided by Parliament is paid in such sums on such conditions as the Secretary of State may, with the approval of the Treasury, recommend towards the expenses of any youthful offender or child detained in a certified school, including the expenses of removal or transfer from one school to another and towards the expenses of disposing of any such offender or child by emigration

[1] Sec. 65   [2] Sec 72   [3] Sec 85

The contribution may not exceed 2s. per head per week for children detained in an industrial school on the application of their parents or guardians.[1]

Duties and Powers of Local Authorities with Respect to Maintenance, etc., of Inmates of Certified Schools.

Where a youthful offender or child is ordered to be sent to a certified reformatory school or to a certified industrial school, it is the duty of the council of the county or county borough in which he resides (to be specified in the order) to provide for his reception and maintenance in a certified reformatory or industrial school, as the case may be.

For the purposes of the foregoing provisions, a youthful offender or child shall be presumed to reside in the place where the offence was committed, or the circumstances which rendered him liable to be sent to a certified school occurred, unless it is proved that he resided in some other place.

Where the Court by which the detention order is made is a Court of assize or a Court of quarter sessions, the Court shall remit to a Court of summary jurisdiction for the place where the youthful offender or child was committed for trial the determination of his place of residence.

The obligation to contribute towards the maintenance of a child in an industrial school imposed on a local education authority shall not apply in the case of a child sent to a certified industrial school—

(a) at the desire of his parent or guardian as being a child whom the parent or guardian is unable to control; or

(b) at the instance of the guardians of the poor law union or the managers of a district poor law school as being a refractory child, or as being the child of parents either of whom has been convicted of an offence punishable with penal servitude or imprisonment; or

(c) being a child who had no settled place of abode and who habitually wandered from place to place through the districts of various local education authorities; or

(d) in respect of whose maintenance in a certified school no contribution is paid out of moneys provided by Parliament.

[1] Sec. 73

But the local education authority may, if they think fit, contribute towards the maintenance of a child in a certified school in any such case.

Education Authority to be Heard.

An order for the detention of a child in a certified industrial school shall not be made by a petty sessional Court unless the local education authority, which by virtue of the order are responsible for providing for the reception and maintenance of the child in a certified school, have been given an opportunity of being heard

Where a local authority, that is to say, as respects reformatory schools the council of a county or county borough, and as respects industrial schools a local education authority, are aggrieved by the decision of a Court as to the place of residence of a youthful offender or child, they may within three months after the making of the detention order apply to a petty sessional Court acting in and for the place for which the Court which made the order or determined the place of residence acted, and that Court, on proof to its satisfaction that the youthful offender or child was resident in the area of another local authority, and after giving such other local authority an opportunity of being heard, may transfer the liability to maintain the youthful offender or child in a certified school to that other local authority, and may order that other local authority to repay to the first-mentioned local authority any expenses incurred by them in respect of the youthful offender or child under the detention order, and an appeal shall lie from the decision of the Court to a Court of quarter sessions; but the liability of the first-mentioned local authority under the detention order is not affected until an order has been made transferring the liability to another local authority

For the purpose of the performance of their duties as to reception and maintenance a local authority—

(a) may contract with the managers of any certified school for the reception and maintenance therein of youthful offenders or children for whose reception and maintenance the authority are required under this section to make provision;

(b) may, with the approval of the Secretary of State, undertake or combine with any other authority in undertaking, or contribute such sums of money upon such conditions as they think fit, towards the establishment, building, alteration, enlargement, rebuilding, or management of a certified school, or the purchase of any land required for the use of an existing certified school, or for the site of any school intended to be a certified school

A local authority may contribute towards the ultimate disposal of any inmate of a certified school for whose maintenance in such a school the authority are under this section responsible, or towards whose maintenance the authority have voluntarily contributed.

The local authority responsible for the maintenance of a youthful offender or child in a certified school under this section shall continue responsible for his maintenance in the event of his transfer to another certified school, notwithstanding that having been originally ordered to be sent to a reformatory school he is subsequently transferred to an industrial school, or having been originally ordered to be sent to an industrial school he is subsequently transferred to, or ordered by a Court to be sent to, a reformatory school, that is, the education authority must maintain a child transferred to a reformatory if he was originally sent to an industrial school Before any such youthful offender or child is ordered to be transferred from one school to another, notice shall be given to the local authority responsible for his maintenance, and that authority shall be given an opportunity of making representations to the Secretary of State with respect thereto [1]

Guardians' Contributions.

Where a child has been ordered to be sent to a certified industrial school at the instance of the guardians of a poor law union or the managers of a district poor law school as refractory, or as the child of parents either of whom has been convicted of an offence punishable with penal servitude or imprisonment, the guardians or managers shall contribute towards the maintenance of the child in a certified industrial school such sums as may be agreed upon between them and the managers of the certified school to which the child is ordered to be sent, or in default of agreement as may be fixed by the Secretary of State

Land may be acquired by a local authority for the purpose of supplying reformatory schools, under and in accordance with the

[1] See 74 (10).

Local Government Act, 1888, in the case of the council of a county, and as for the purposes of the Public Health Acts in the case of the council of a county borough; and for the purpose of supplying industrial schools, as for the purpose of the Education Acts, 1870 to 1907.

The expenses incurred by a local authority in this matter shall be defrayed—

(a) as respects reformatory schools, as expenses for general county purposes in the case of the council of a county, and out of the borough fund or borough rate in the case of the council of a county borough;

(b) as respects industrial schools, as expenses incurred for the purposes of elementary education.

Money may be borrowed by a local authority for the purposes of defraying or contributing towards the expenses of establishing, building, altering, enlarging, rebuilding, or purchasing land for the use or site of—

(a) a reformatory school under and in accordance with the Local Government Act, 1888, in the case of the council of a county, and under and in accordance with the Municipal Corporations Act, 1882, in the case of the council of a county borough;

(b) an industrial school, under and in accordance with the Education Acts, 1870 to 1907;

provided that the maximum period within which money so borrowed is to be repaid shall be sixty years.

Local education authorities, with the approval of the Secretary of State, may agree to combine for these purposes; the agreement may provide for the appointment of a joint body of managers, and for the apportionment of the contributions to be paid by each authority and any other matters which, in the opinion of the Secretary of State, are necessary for carrying out the agreement, and the expenses of any such joint body of managers shall be paid in the proportions specified in the agreement by each of the authorities, and their receipts and payments shall be audited in manner provided by section 6 of the Education (Administrative Provisions) Act, 1907.[1]

[1] 7 Ed. VII, Ch. 43.

Contributions by Parents.

The parent or other person liable to maintain a youthful offender or child ordered to be sent to and detained in a certified school shall, if able to do so, contribute to his maintenance therein a sum not exceeding such sum as may be declared by Order in Council to represent approximately the average cost of maintenance of youthful offenders or children in the class of school to which such school belongs in the locality in which such school is situate

The Court by which a detention order is made shall, at the time of making that order, or any petty sessional Court having jurisdiction at the place where such parent or other person resides may, on complaint being made by, or at the instance of, the chief inspector of reformatory and industrial schools, at any time whilst the offender or child is detained in the school, make an order on such parent or other person for the payment to the chief inspector of such weekly sum, not exceeding such sum aforesaid, as having regard to the ability of the parent or other person seems reasonable during the whole or any part of the time for which the offender or child is liable to be detained in the school. The payment of such sum may be remitted by the Secretary of State [1]

If the Court making the detention order is a Court of assize or Court of quarter sessions it may, if it thinks fit, remit the case to a Court of summary jurisdiction for the place where the offender or child was committed for trial, for the purpose of making an order under this section, and upon the case being so remitted any such Court of summary jurisdiction shall have power to make any such order under this section as the Court which made the detention order might have made

Every such order may specify the time during which the payment is to be made, or may direct the payment to be made until further notice, and shall be enforceable as if it were an order of affiliation

Such orders may, on application being made either by the person on whom the order is made or by or at the instance of the chief inspector and on fourteen days' notice of such application being given to the chief inspector or person on whom the order was made, be varied by any Court which would have had power to make the order

[1] Sec 75, Children Act, 1908.

If the person on whom the order is made was not summoned to attend the sitting of the Court at which the order was made, the order shall be served on him in manner prescribed by rules of Court, and shall be binding on him unless he makes an application against it within the time prescribed by rules of Court to the Court by which the order was made or any Court of like jurisdiction on the ground either that he is not liable to maintain the offender or child, or that he is unable to contribute the sum specified in the order. On any such application being made the Court may confirm the order with or without modifications or may rescind it.

Where a parent or other person has been ordered to contribute to the maintenance of a youthful offender or child, he shall give notice of any change of address of the child to the inspector of reformatory and industrial schools, and if he fails to do so without reasonable excuse, he shall be liable on summary conviction to a fine not exceeding £2.

All sums received as maintenance shall be paid into the Exchequer, but if the amount received in respect of any child in an industrial school exceeds the contribution from the Treasury in respect of that child, the excess shall be paid to the managers of the school and shall not be paid into the Exchequer.

It shall be the duty of a constable, if so required by the chief inspector of reformatory and industrial schools, to take proceedings under this section on behalf of the chief inspector.[1]

Where there is a person other than the parent liable to maintain the youthful offender or child, an order under this section may be made on that person notwithstanding there may be also a parent.

Any Court making an order for contribution by a parent or other such person may, in any case where there is any pension or income payable to such parent or other person and capable of being attached, after giving the person by whom the pension or income is payable an opportunity of being heard, further order that such part as the Court may see fit of the pension or income be attached and be paid to the person named by the Court. Such further order shall be an authority to the person by whom such pension or income is payable to make the payment so ordered. The receipt of the

[1] Sec. 75 (9)

person to whom payment is ordered shall be a good discharge to such first-named person.[1]

Expenses of Conveyance and Clothing.

The expense of conveying to any certified reformatory school any youthful offender who has been directed to be detained in such a school, and the expense of proper clothing for him requisite for his admission to the school, shall be defrayed out of moneys provided by Parliament.[2]

The expense of conveying to a certified industrial school a child ordered to be sent there shall be defrayed by the police authority by whom he is conveyed, and shall be deemed part of the current expenses of that authority; but where a child is committed to a certified industrial school at the instance of a local education authority, the authority may pay the expenses of and incidental to the conveyance of the child to and from the school and the sending of the child out on licence and bringing back the child on the revocation or forfeiture of the licence.[3]

Day Industrial Schools

Establishment, etc, of Day Industrial Schools.

If the Secretary of State is satisfied that, owing to the circumstances of any class of population in the area of any local education authority, a school in which industrial training, elementary education, and one or more meals a day, but not lodging, are provided, is necessary or expedient for the proper training and control of the children of that class, he may, on the like application and report as is required by section 45 of the Children Act in the case of industrial schools, certify any such school as a day industrial school, as fit for the reception of children to be sent there in pursuance of the provisions relating to day industrial schools, so that such school shall be deemed to be a certified efficient school within the meaning of the Elementary Education Act, 1876.[4]

A school shall not at the same time be a day industrial school and a reformatory or industrial school

If the Secretary of State is of opinion that, by reason of a change

---

[1] Sec 75   [2] Sec 76   [3] Sec 76
[4] 39 and 40 Vict., Ch 79

of circumstances or otherwise, a certified day industrial school ceases to be necessary or expedient for the proper training and control of the children of any class of population in the neighbourhood of that school, he may, after due notice, withdraw the certificate of the school, and thereupon the school shall cease to be a certified day industrial school.

Power to send Children to Day Industrial Schools.

Any child authorised to be sent to a certified industrial school may, if the Court before which the child is brought thinks it expedient, be sent to a certified day industrial school

Any child sent to a certified day industrial school by an order of a Court (other than an attendance order) may, during the period specified in the order, be there detained during such hours as may be authorised by the rules of the school approved by the Secretary of State.

The school must be within such distance of the residence of the child as may be prescribed by Order in Council, but need not be situate within the jurisdiction of the Court making the order.[1]

Reception of Child under Attendance Order or Without Order.

The managers of a certified day industrial school may, upon the request of a local education authority and of the parent or guardian of, or other person legally liable to maintain a child, and upon the undertaking of the parent, guardian, or other person to pay towards the industrial training and meals of the child such sum as the Secretary of State may authorise, receive the child into the school under an attendance order or without an order of a Court [2]

Contributions by the Treasury.

There shall be paid out of the money provided by Parliament towards the custody, industrial training, elementary education, and meals of children sent to a day industrial school such sums, on such conditions, as the Secretary of State, with the approval of the Treasury, may recommend—

Provided that—

(a) the conditions of a Parliamentary contribution to a day industrial school shall provide that the education given in the

[1] Sec 78   [2] Sec 79

school shall be on such a level of efficiency as would enable the school, if a public elementary school, to obtain a parliamentary grant ,

(*b*) any conditions recommended by the Secretary of State for the purposes of contributions to a day industrial school shall be laid before Parliament in the same manner as minutes of the Board of Education relating to the annual Parliamentary grant.

Powers of Local Education Authorities.

A local education authority shall have the same powers in relation to a certified day industrial school as it has in relation to a certified industrial school, but this does not impose on any such authority an obligation to provide for the reception and maintenance of a child in a certified day industrial school [1]

Contributions by Parents.

The Court shall also order the parent of the child, or other person liable to maintain him, to contribute to his industrial training and meals in the school such sum as may be declared by Order in Council to represent approximately the average cost of industrial training and meals in day industrial schools in the locality in which the school to which the child is sent is situate

It shall be the duty of the local education authority to obtain and enforce the order, and every sum paid under the order shall be paid over to the local education authority in aid of their expenses for elementary education under the Education Acts, 1870 to 1907

If a parent or other person is unable to pay the sum required by the order to be paid, he shall apply to the guardians of the poor law union comprising the parish in which the parent or other person is resident, who, if satisfied of such liability, shall give the parent or other person sufficient relief to pay the sum, or so much thereof as they consider him unable to pay. [2]

Various points relating to education may be more fully considered in relation to the provisions as to employment, and further information is, therefore, reserved for the next chapter Further amendment of the law with respect to the treatment and punishment of young offenders in relation to training is provided in the Criminal Justice Administration Act, 1914 [3]

---

[1] Sec 81   [2] Sec 82
[3] 4 & 5 Geo V, Ch 58, Secs 7–11   (Sec 10 comes into force 1st Sept , 1915)

CHAPTER IX

RESTRICTIONS ON THE EMPLOYMENT OF CHILDREN AND YOUNG PERSONS

THE attitude of the law towards the employment of children in Blackstone's day was in no way against employment. Indeed, in his short paragraph[1] on parental duty to educate, he mentions one instance of " a wise provision for breeding up the rising generation ; since the poor and laborious part of the community, when past the age of nurture, are taken out of the hands of their parents by the statutes[2] for apprenticing poor children."

Since Blackstone's day the attitude of the law has distinctly changed, and the Factory Acts in conjunction with various Education Acts have conduced to remarkable changes in the outlook of children.

Whilst the Education Act of 1870[3] did make provision for the attendance of children at school, it made no provision against the employment of children. The defect of the Act in this direction was remedied by the Act of 1876.[4]

After providing that it is the duty of the parent of every child to cause it to receive efficient elementary instruction in reading, writing, and arithmetic,[5] the Elementary Education Act, 1876, provides that a person shall not, after the commencement of this Act, take into his employment any child who is not of the age of ten years, or being of the age of ten has not obtained a certificate of proficiency in reading, writing, and arithmetic, or of previous due attendance at a certified efficient school, unless such child, being of the age of ten years or upwards, is employed and is attending school in accordance with the provisions of the Factory Acts or of any by-law of the local authority made under section 74 of the Elementary Education Act, 1870, or amendments thereto.[6] The age limit of ten years has now been extended by the Elementary

---
[1] *Commentaries*, I, p 451
[2] Stat 5 Eliz, Ch 2, 1 James I, Ch 25, 7 James I, Ch 3
[3] 33 and 34 Vict, Ch 75, Sec 74
[4] Elem Ed Act, 1876, 39 and 40 Vict., Ch 79
[5] Sec 4   [6] Sec 5, see p 65

Education Act, 1893,[1] and, further, by the Elementary Education Act (1893) Amendment Act, 1899,[2] to twelve years subject to exceptions as to employment in agricultural labour which are made in the latter Act.[3] Every person who takes a child into his employment in contravention of the provisions of these Acts is liable on summary conviction to a penalty not exceeding 40s[4] As to the standards of proficiency in reading, writing, and arithmetic or of previous due attendance at a certified efficient school, the First Schedule of the Act of 1876 fixes the standard as that of Standard IV of the Code of 1876, which, so far as reading, writing, and arithmetic are concerned, is the reading of a passage from a reading book or history of England, the writing of eight lines of poetry or prose slowly read once and then dictated, and compound rules (money) and reduction of common weights and measures in arithmetic The standard may be a higher standard than this. The Board of Education Regulations issued on 21st March, 1901, provide that any child over the age of twelve years, or if the child is employed in agriculture under any by-law made under section 1 of the Elementary Education Act (1893) Amendment Act, 1899, over eleven years of age shall be admitted to an examination for a certificate of proficiency on the application of the child's parent, guardian, or the local authority. The inspector may only refuse to examine where due provision has already been made for the child's examination elsewhere, or the child has not received at least six months' instruction in the standard in which he is presented or has already failed at an examination held within three months Certificates of proficiency are granted by means of a schedule directed to the managers of the school or local authority, such schedule containing the names of all children who have attained the requisite standard

The standard of previous due attendance is now 350 attendances per year for any five years after the child has attained five years of age, and made in not more than two schools.[5]

In the case of children to be employed in agriculture as above mentioned, thirteen years may be fixed by the by-laws as the minimum age for exemption from attendance at school. Where such provision is made, such children over eleven and under thirteen

---
[1] 56 and 57 Vict, Ch 51.   [2] 62 and 63 Vict, Ch. 13.
[3] See pp 80 and 118   [4] Sec. 6.
[5] 39 and 40 Vict, Ch 79, Sec 5, and Schedule 1 amended by 63 and 64 Vict., Ch. 53, Sec. 9

years of age who have passed the standard fixed by the by-laws,[1] are not required to attend school more than 250 times a year.

Section 6 of the Elementary Education Act, 1900, substitutes fourteen for thirteen years in section 74 of the Education Act, 1870, and section 4 of the Elementary Education Act, 1880, relating to the making of by-laws relative to compulsory attendance at school, but this amending section does not affect the proviso in section 1 of the Elementary Education (School Attendance) Act (1893) Amendment Act, 1899, whereby a local education authority may by by-law fix the age of thirteen as the minimum age for exemption from school attendance in the case of children to be employed in agriculture and of between eleven and thirteen for partial exemption A person, therefore, taking a child into full time employment in agriculture commits no offence under the Elementary Education Act, 1876,[2] although the child is not of such educational standard as to entitle him to total exemption under the age of fourteen[3] provided the provision of the Act of 1899 is not offended.

Under section 74 of the Elementary Education Act, 1870, as amended by section 4 of the Elementary Education Act, 1880, a school board[4] may make by-laws regulating compulsory attendance of children under thirteen years of age. This age has been raised to fourteen years[5] with a result that section 4 of the Education Act, 1880, so amended will read—

" Every person who takes into his employment a child of the age of ten and under the age of fourteen years before that child has obtained a certificate of having reached the standard of education fixed by a by-law in force in the district for the total or partial exemption of children of the like age from the obligation to attend school, shall be deemed to take such child into his employment in contravention of the Elementary Education Act, 1876, and shall be liable to a penalty accordingly. In the case of a child who, under the by-laws,[6] is required to attend school full time, any person employing a child so that he is unable to comply with the by-laws has contravened the provisions of section 5 of the Act of 1876 "

This section, therefore, must be read in conjunction with the provisions of the Factory and Workshop Act, 1901.[7] It has been

[1] See Education
[2] Sec 5
[3] *Strong* v *Treise* (1909), 1 K B 613, 100 L T R. 340
[4] Now Local Education Authority
[5] 63 and 64 Vict, Ch 53, Sec 6
[6] See Education, p 79
[7] Secs 68 to 71

laid down[1] that the Education Acts do not control the provisions of the Factory Act regulating the education of children employed in accordance with that Act. In *Mellor* v *Denham*, a child, although not complying with the by-laws, was regularly attending an efficient elementary school pursuant to the Factory and Workshop Act, 1878, and the Divisional Court held that the by-laws could not be enforced where a child between ten and thirteen years was attending an efficient elementary school and observing the conditions of the Factory and Workshop Act, although not obeying the by-laws. The collision thus threatened between the labour provisions of the Factory Act and the school attendance provisions in the by-laws was, therefore, averted by the adoption of an attendance qualification for exemption in the case of children over thirteen.[2] A more recent decision on the construction of by-laws and their effect in conjunction with sections 68 to 71 of the Factory and Workshop Act, 1901, is *Stevenson* v *Goldstraw*.[3]

Factory Act

The main provisions with regard to education and employment of children contained in the Factory and Workshop Act, 1901, are as follows—

"A child under the age of twelve must not be employed in a factory or workshop[4] and every child over that age must first have a certificate of fitness for employment which shall state among other things that the certifying surgeon is satisfied that the person named therein is of the age stated.[5] The evidence of age required is the production of a certificate of birth being a certified copy of the entry in the register of births of the birth of the young person or child in question, or a certificate from a local education authority founded on returns transmitted to that authority by the registrar of births and deaths under the provisions of section 26 of the Elementary Education Act, 1876."

Where the age of a child is required for any purpose connected with education or employment in labour, a certified copy of the entry of the child's birth in the register may be obtained at a fee not exceeding 1s. by presentation of a written requisition in the

---

[1] *Mellor* v *Denham*, 4 Q B D 241 ; 40 L T R 395
[2] Board of Education Report, 1901-2
[3] (1906) 2 K.B 298 ; 95 L T R 111 See pp 121-2 *infra*
[4] Sec. 62.　　[5] Secs 63 and 64

prescribed form.[1] Section 134 of the Factory Act, however, fixes the fee at 6d, and the age limit of the person on whose behalf the certificate is applied is raised to sixteen, and the penny inland revenue stamp is not required to be fixed to these certificates [2]

Where a child (i.e, a person under the age of fourteen years and who has not, being of the age of thirteen years, obtained a certificate of proficiency or attendance at school as required by Part III [3] of the Factory and Workshop Act) is employed in a factory or workshop, its parent must cause it to attend some recognised efficient school for one attendance at least on each work-day in any week during any part of which he is employed, or if employed on alternate days, he must make two attendances on each day preceding a day of employment [4]

No child, however, is required to attend school on Saturday or on a holiday or half-holiday allowed in the factory or workshop in which is he employed, nor will his attendance be required when prevented by sickness or other unavoidable cause or when the school is closed for holidays If there is not within two miles, measured by the nearest road from the child's residence, a recognised efficient school, it will be sufficient if the child attends a school not recognised if such school is temporarily approved in writing by an inspector [5] A child who, in any week, fails to make the required attendances at school must not be employed until he has made up the deficiency by attendance at school during the following week.

The two expressions "certified efficient school" and "recognised efficient school" are defined in the following terms—

"Certified efficient school" means a public elementary school within the meaning of the Elementary Education Acts, 1870 to 1900, and any workhouse school in England certified to be efficient by the local government board and any elementary school which is not conducted for private profit and is open at all reasonable times to the inspection of His Majesty's Inspectors of Schools, and requires the like attendance from its scholars as is required in a public elementary school, and keeps such registers of those attendances as are for the time being required by the Board

---

[1] 39 and 40 Vict., Ch 79, Sec 25
[2] 54 and 55 Vict, Ch. 39 (Schedule)
[3] Sec. 71   [4] 1 Ed. VII, Ch 22, Sec. 68.   [5] Ibid

of Education and is certified by the Board to be an efficient school.[1]

"Recognised efficient school" means a certified efficient school, and any school which the Board of Education have not refused to take into consideration under the Elementary Education Act, 1870, as a school giving efficient elementary education to, and suitable for, the children of the school district and which is recognised for the time being by an Inspector under the Education Act as giving efficient elementary education. An Inspector who recognises any school as efficient must make a report to that effect forthwith to the Board of Education

The power to make by-laws under section 74 of the Elementary Education Act, 1870, is now a *duty* which every education authority must carry out.[2] Model by-laws[3] have been issued by the Board of Education, and these should be closely followed; it is not necessary, however, to provide by-laws for the partial exemption of children from the obligation to attend school. Where, however, no provision is made, a child of the age of twelve who has attained a certificate of previous due attendance at a certified efficient school may, under section 68 of the Factory and Workshop Act, 1901, be employed as a half-timer in a factory or workshop notwithstanding the fact that the local education authority have made no provision in their by-laws for the partial exemption of children from the obligation to attend school.[4] The employment of a child of thirteen in a factory or workshop is subject to his having received a certificate of proficiency in reading, writing, and arithmetic of such standard as is fixed by the Secretary of State with the consent of the Board of Education; by order of the Secretary of State this is fixed as that of the fifth standard or any higher standard named in the by-laws of the local education authority. Alternatively, a certificate of previous due attendance at a certified efficient school will be sufficient, *i.e.*, a certificate that the child, between the ages of five and thirteen, has made 350 attendances during each year for five years, not necessarily consecutive, in not more than two schools.[5] This provision does not, however, give authority for

---

[1] 1 Ed VII, Ch 22, Sec 72, and Rules of the Board of Education, dated April, 1902.   [2] 43 and 44 Vict, Ch 23, Sec 2 (see Education)
[3] See p 79, Education.
[4] *Stevenson* v *Goldstraw*, 1906, 2 K B 298; 95 L T R 111
[5] 1 Ed VII, Ch 22, Sec 71.

the *full time* employment of a child of thirteen who has obtained a certificate of previous due attendance or proficiency in reading, writing, and arithmetic at a certified efficient school unless provision is made by the local education authority in their by-law for the total exemption of such a child from the obligation to attend school.[1] The provisions of the Factory and Workshop Act extend to laundries, i e , so far as the education and employment of children is concerned.

Where a child is employed half-time the teacher of the school at which he attends must once in each week give a certificate of the child's attendance during the previous week to the occupier of a factory or workshop which certificate must be kept by the occupier for two months and produced to an Inspector whenever required during that period. If a child is employed during any week without such certificate of his previous due attendance being in the hands of his employer, he is employed contrary to the Act.[2] Factory Inspectors have power to inspect at any time factories or workshops when they have reasonable cause to believe that a person is employed therein, and they may enter by day any place which they reasonably believe to be a factory or workshop; they have similar powers of entering a school in which they have cause to believe children employed in a factory or workshop are for the time being educated and to examine such children with respect to any matter under the Factory Act

Employer's Liability.

Where any person is employed in a factory or workshop other than a domestic factory or workshop, contrary to the provisions of the Factory Act, the occupier of the factory or workshop is liable to a fine not exceeding £3, or if the offence was committed by night £5 for each person so employed, and in the case of a second or subsequent conviction in relation to a factory within two years from the last conviction for the same offence not less than £1 for each offence, and where any person is so employed in a domestic factory or workshop the occupier shall be liable to a fine not exceeding £1, or if the offence was committed by night £2 for each person so employed, and in the case of a second or subsequent conviction

---

[1] *Stevenson v Goldstraw*, 1906, 2 K B 298, 95 L T R 111
[2] Sec. 69, Factory Act, 1901

within two years from the last conviction in relation to a factory for the same offence not less than £1 for each offence.[1]

Parent's Liability.

Where an offence is in relation to a child or young person, the parent of such child or young person is also liable to a fine not exceeding 20s. for each offence unless the Court is satisfied that the offence was committed without the consent, connivance, or wilful default of the parent; or if the parent neglects to cause the child to attend school in accordance with the Factory Act, a similar penalty may be inflicted for each offence.[2]

The penalty for employing a child in contravention of section 5 of the Elementary Education Act, 1876, is a fine not exceeding 40s.

Employment by a Parent

A parent of a child who employs such child in any labour exercised by way of trade or for the purpose of gain shall be deemed to have employed the child "or taken the child into his employment" within the meaning of section 5 of the Elementary Education Act, 1876.[3]

What is "Taking into Employment."

A father keeping his child at home for domestic purposes in order that his wife may go out to work and earn money, has no reasonable excuse within section 11 of the Act, but on the other hand, he has not employed the child "for purposes of gain" and cannot be liable to conviction under section 6 of the Act.[4]

Where a child of thirteen was in delicate health and subject to fits, and the parents, acting on medical advice, detained the child at home, allowing him to go into the father's workshop at will and do what work he was minded to do, the father was held not to have taken the child into his employment contrary to the Act.[5]

Time Limit.

By virtue of the Employment of Children Act, 1903,[6] general restrictions on employment of children are laid down. It is there

---

[1] 1 Ed. VII, Ch. 22, Sec. 137. [2] Sec. 138, ibid.
[3] See Sec. 47, 39 and 40 Vict., Ch. 79.
[4] *Mather v. Lawrence* (1899), 1 Q.B. 1,000; 80 L.T.R. 600.
[5] *Rex v. Austin Ex parte Leah*, 96 L.T. 29; 71 J.P. 29.
[6] 3 Ed. VII, Ch. 45, Sec. 3.

provided that no child (that is, a person under fourteen years of age) shall be employed between the hours of nine in the evening and six[1] in the morning. These hours may be varied by the by-laws of any local authority either as regards employment generally or in certain specified trades. The proper authority to make such by-laws is the county council, except in urban districts with a population of over 20,000 according to the census of 1901 and in boroughs having a population of 10,000, in which cases the by-laws are made by the respective district and borough councils.

Street Trading.

No child under the age of eleven years may be employed in street trading,[2] and a local authority as above defined[3] may make by-laws in relation to street trading by persons under sixteen years of age.[4] For the special protection of girls the local authority should, in making such by-laws, have special regard to the desirability of preventing the employment of girls under sixteen in streets or public places.[5] The by-laws in respect to young persons may—

(a) prohibit street trading subject to exceptions as to age, sex, or otherwise as may be specified in the by-law, or subject to the holding of a licence to trade to be granted by the authority;

(b) regulate the conditions on which licences may be granted, suspended, and revoked;

(c) determine the days and hours during which, and the places at which, such street trading may be carried on;

(d) require such street traders to wear badges; and

(e) regulate generally the conduct of such street traders, provided that in granting licences or limiting the right to trade no condition having reference to the poverty or general bad character of a person claiming to trade or applying for a licence may be made.

No child shall be employed in any other occupation who is already employed as a half-timer under the Factory and Workshop Act, 1901.[6]

---

[1] But as to Mines see 1 and 2 Geo V, Ch 50, Sec 92, and p 132 *infra*
[2] 3 Ed VII, Ch 45, Sec 3 (2)   [3] 3 Ed VII, Ch 45, Sec 13
[4] *Ibid*, Sec 2   [5] *Ibid*, Sec 2 (2)
[6] Employment of Children Act, 1903, Sec 3 (3)

Injurious Occupations.

A child shall not be employed to lift, carry, or move anything so heavy as to be likely to cause injury to the child,[1] nor shall such child be employed in any occupation likely to be injurious to his life, limb, health, or education, regard being had to his or her physical condition[2]

In respect to such employment likely to injure or undermine the child's constitution the local authority may notify an employer of a child by sending a certificate signed by a registered medical practitioner intimating that the lifting, carrying, or moving of any specified weight is likely to cause injury to the child or that any specified occupation is likely to be injurious to the life, limb, health, or education of the child Should any steps be taken against an employer in respect of improper employment of such child subsequently, any such certificate will be admissible as evidence against the employer.[3]

General By-laws.

A local authority may make by-laws specifying the age below which employment of children under fourteen is illegal, the hours within which employment is illegal and the number of daily and weekly hours beyond which employment of such children is illegal They may also prohibit employment of such children in any specified occupation or allow employment subject to conditions.[4] Special provision as to sex may be made under this section of the Act

By-laws, when Binding.

By-laws under the Employment of Children Act, 1903, are binding only when confirmed by the Secretary of State, which confirmation only takes place after thirty days after the publication of the by-laws as ordered by the Secretary of State[5] The publication and following period of thirty days is provided in order that any objection may be made by persons likely to be affected Such objections will be considered by the Secretary of State who may order a local inquiry at the expense of the authority framing the by-law

---

[1] *Ibid*, Sec 3 (4), also as to Coal Mines 1 and 2 Geo V, Ch 50, Sec 92 (7) *infra*, p 132
[2] *Ibid*, Sec 3 (5) [3] *Ibid*, Sec 3 (6)
[4] *Ibid*, Sec 1   [5] *Ibid*, Sec 4

Offences and Penalties.

The Act provides that—[1]

"(1) If any person employs a child or other person under the age of sixteen in contravention of this Act, or of any by-law under the Act, he shall be liable on summary conviction to a fine not exceeding forty shillings, or, in the case of a second or subsequent offence, not exceeding five pounds;

"(2) If any parent or guardian of a child or other person under the age of sixteen has conduced to the commission of the alleged offence by wilful default, or by habitually neglecting to exercise due care, he shall be liable on summary conviction to the like fine;

"(3) If any person under the age of sixteen contravenes the provisions of any by-law as to street trading made under this Act, he shall be liable on summary conviction to a fine not exceeding twenty shillings, and in case of a second or subsequent offence, if a child, to be sent to an industrial school, and if not a child, to a fine not exceeding five pounds:

"(4) In lieu of ordering a child to be sent under this section to an industrial school, a Court of summary jurisdiction may order the child to be taken out of the charge or control of the person who actually has the charge or control of the child, and to be committed to the charge and control of some fit person who is willing to undertake the same until such child reaches the age of sixteen years. The provisions of sections 7 and 8 of the Prevention of Cruelty to Children Act, 1894,[2] shall, with the necessary modifications, apply to any order for the disposal of a child made under this sub-section."

Offences by Agents or Workmen and by Parents.

By section 6 where the offence of taking a child into employment in contravention of this Act is, in fact, committed by an agent or workman of the employer, such agent or workman shall be liable to a penalty as if he were the employer.

Where a child is taken into employment in contravention of this Act on the production, by or with the privity of the parent, of a forged or false certificate, or on the false representation of his parent that the child is of an age at which such employment is not in contravention of this Act, that parent shall be liable to a penalty not exceeding 40s.

Where an employer is charged with any offence under this Act, he shall be entitled, upon information duly laid by him, to have

---

[1] *Ibid*, Sec 5   [2] Now Children Act, 1908 Sec. 21

any other person whom he charges[1] as the actual offender brought before the Court at the time appointed for hearing the charge, and if, after the commission of the offence has been proved, the Court is satisfied that the employer had used diligence to comply with the provisions of the Act, and that the other person had committed the offence in question without the employer's knowledge, consent, or connivance, the other person shall be summarily convicted of the offence, and the employer shall be exempt from any fine

When it is made to appear to the satisfaction of an Inspector or other officer charged with the enforcement of this Act, at the time of discovering the offence, that the employer had used all due diligence to enforce compliance with this Act, and also by what person the offence had been committed, and also that it had been committed without the knowledge, consent, or connivance of the employer, and in contravention of his order, then the Inspector or officer shall proceed against the person whom he believes to be the actual offender in the first instance without first proceeding against the employer.

Council By-law.

A by-law made by a local authority under the Employment of Children Act, 1903, was to the effect that no child, liable to attend school full time should, on days when the school was open, be employed between 8 30 a m and 5 p m

Employer's Liability.

In *Robinson* (app) v *Hill* (resp)[2] the respondent was summoned under the by-law for unlawfully employing a child between the hours in question The child, liable to be at school full time, was employed during prohibited hours in delivering bread to respondent's customers, for a vanman in respondent's service The vanman engaged the child and paid his wages, and the engagement was no part of the vanman's contract with his employer The respondent knew that the child was employed in delivering bread but only in permitted hours The Court held that respondent was not liable as an employer, and that to bring a person within the

---

[1] *Robinson* v *Hill* (1910), 1 K B 94, and 101 L I R 573
[2] (1910) 1 K B 94, and 101 L T R 573

Act there must purport to be a contract of employment between the person charged and the child. It was further laid down that a person so charged was under no compulsion to charge any other person[1] as a condition precedent to his own dismissal from the charge

Limitation of Time.

With respect to summary proceedings for offences and fines under this Act, and any by-laws made thereunder, the information shall be laid within three months after the commission of the offence [2]

Power of Officer of Local Authority to Enter Place of Employment.

If it appear to any justice of the peace on the complaint of an officer of the local authority acting under this Act, that there is reasonable cause to believe that a child is employed in contravention of the Act in any place, whether a building or not, such justice may, by order under his hand, empower an officer of the local authority to enter such place at any reasonable time, within forty-eight hours from the date of the order, and examine such place and any person therein touching the employment of any child therein [3]

Any person refusing admission to an officer authorised by an order under this section, or obstructing him in the discharge of his duty, shall, for each offence, be liable on summary conviction to a penalty not exceeding £20

Employment in Factories, 35 and 36 Vict., Ch. 77, 50 and 51 Vict., Ch. 58, 1 Ed. VII, Ch. 22.

By-laws made under this Act shall not apply to any child above 12 employed in pursuance of the Factory and Workshop Act, 1901, or the Metalliferous Mines Regulation Act, 1872, or the Coal Mines Regulation Act, 1887,[4] so far as regards that employment ; and in the application of section 3 to children employed under those Acts the Inspectors appointed under those Acts shall be substituted for the local authority in respect of such employment. [5]

---

[1] See Sec 6, ss 3, Employment of Children Act, 1903, 3 Ed VII, Ch 45, *supra*, p 126
[2] 3 Ed VII, Ch 45, Sec 7   [3] *Ibid*, Sec 8
[4] Now Coal Mines Act, 1911, 1 and 2 Geo. V, Ch 50, Secs 91 and 92
[5] 3 Ed VII, Ch 45 Sec 9.

Saving for Industrial and Other Schools.

Nothing in this Act or in any by-law made thereunder shall apply to the exercise of manual labour by any child under order of detention in a certified industrial or reformatory school, or by any child while receiving instruction in manual labour in any school [1]

Expenses of Act in England and Wales.

Any expenses incurred by a local authority in England and Wales in carrying into effect the provisions of this Act or any by-law made thereunder shall be defrayed in the case of a county out of the county fund, and in the case of a borough out of the borough fund or borough rate, and in the case of any other urban district out of any rate or fund applicable for defraying expenses incurred in the execution of the Public Health Acts provided that a county council shall not raise any sum on account of their expenses under this Act within any borough or urban district the council of which is a local authority under this Act [2]

Definitions.

The following expressions used in the Employment of Children Act, 1903, are defined in section 13—

" Child " means a person under the age of fourteen years ;

" Guardian," used in reference to a child, includes any person who is liable to maintain or has the actual custody of the child;

" Employ " and " employment," used in reference to a child, include employment in any labour exercised by way of trade or for the purposes of gain,[3] whether the gain be to the child or to any other person,

" Local authority " means, in the case of the City of London, the mayor, aldermen, and commons of that city in common council assembled, in the case of a municipal borough with a population according to the census of 1901 of over 10,000, the borough council, and in the case of any other urban district, with a population according to the census of 1901 of over 20,000, the district council, and elsewhere the county council

Meaning of Street Trading.

" Street trading " includes the hawking of newspapers, matches,

---

[1] *Ibid*, Sec 10   [2] Sec 12
[3] *Mather* v *Lawrence* (1899), 1 Q B 1,000, as to construction put upon Sec 47, Elem Ed. Act, 1876

flowers, and other articles; playing, singing, or performing for profit, shoe-blacking, and any other like occupation carried on in streets and public places.

Restrictions on Employment of Children.

By way of the amendment of the Employment of Children Act, 1903, the Prevention of Cruelty to Children Act, 1904, which in this respect is not altered by the Children Act, 1908, provides[1] that if any person—

"(a) causes or procures any child, being a boy under the age of fourteen years, or being a girl under the age of sixteen years, or, having the custody, charge, or care of any such child, allows that child to be in any street, or in any premises licensed for the sale of any intoxicating liquor, other than premises licensed according to law for public entertainments, for the purpose of singing, playing, or performing, or being exhibited for profit, or offering anything for sale, between nine p.m and six a m., or

"(b) causes or procures any child under eleven years, or, having the custody, charge, or care of any such child allows that child to be at any time in any street, or in any premises licensed for the sale of any intoxicating liquor,[2] or in any premises licensed according to law for public entertainments, or in any circus or other place of public amusement to which the public are admitted by payment, for the purpose of singing, playing, or performing, or being exhibited for profit, or offering anything for sale; or

"(c) causes or procures any child under the age of sixteen years, or, having the custody, charge, or care of any such child, allows that child to be in any place for the purpose of being trained as an acrobat, contortionist, or circus performer, or of being trained for any exhibition or performance which in its nature is dangerous,"

that person shall, on summary conviction, be liable at the discretion of the Court, to a fine not exceeding £25, or alternatively, or in default of payment of such fine, or in addition thereto, to imprisonment, with or without hard labour, for any term not exceeding three months

Provided that—

Charity Exempted.

"(1) This section shall not apply in the case of any occasional sale or entertainment the net proceeds of which are wholly applied for the benefit of any school or to any charitable object, if such

---

[1] Sec 2   [2] See also Children Act, 1908, Sec 120

sale or entertainment is held elsewhere than in premises which are licensed for the sale of any intoxicating liquor but not licensed according to law for public entertainments, or if, in the case of a sale or entertainment held in any such premises as aforesaid, a special exemption from the provisions of this section has been granted in writing under the hands of two justices of the peace ; and

" (2) Any local authority may, if it think it necessary or desirable to do so, from time to time by by-law extend or restrict the hours mentioned in paragraph (b) of this section, either on every day or on any specified day or days of the week, and either as to the whole of their district or as to any specified area therein ; and

" (3) Paragraph (c) of this section shall not apply in any case in respect of which a licence granted under this Act is in force, so far as that licence extends "

Licences for Employment of Children.

A petty sessional Court, or in Scotland, the school board, may, notwithstanding anything in this Act, or in the Employment of Children Act, 1903, or any by-laws made thereunder, grant a licence from such time and during such hours of the day, and subject to such restrictions and conditions as the Court or board think fit, for any child exceeding ten years of age—

(a) to take part in any entertainment or series of entertainments to take place in premises licensed according to law for public entertainments, or in any circus or other place of public amusement as aforesaid ; or

(b) to be trained as aforesaid ; or

(c) for both purposes,

if satisfied as to the fitness of the child for the purpose, and if it is shown to their satisfaction that proper provision has been made to secure the health and kind treatment of the children taking part in the entertainment or series of entertainments or being trained as aforesaid, and the Court or board may, upon sufficient cause, vary, add to, or rescind any such licence [1]

Any such licence shall be sufficient protection to all persons acting under or in accordance with the same.

Inspection.

It shall be the duty of Inspectors and other officers charged with the execution of the Employment of Children Act, 1903, to see

---

[1] See also Children (Employment Abroad) Act, 1913 See p 13.

whether the restrictions and conditions of licences are duly complied with, and any such Inspector or officer shall have the same power to enter, inspect, and examine any place of public entertainment at which the employment of a child is for the time being licensed under this section as an Inspector appointed under the Factory and Workshop Act, 1901, has to enter, inspect, and examine a factory or workshop under section 119 of that Act, and that section shall apply accordingly

Where any person applies for a licence, he shall, at least seven days before making the application, give notice thereof to the chief officer of police for the district in which the licence is to take effect, and that officer may appear or instruct some person to appear before the authority hearing the application, and show cause why the licence should not be granted, and the authority to whom the application is made shall not grant the same unless they are satisfied that notice has been properly given.

Where a licence is granted to any person, that person shall forthwith cause a copy thereof to be sent to the local authority for the district in which the licence is to take effect, and if he fails to cause such copy to be sent shall be liable on summary conviction to a fine not exceeding £5.

Nothing in the foregoing rules shall affect the provisions of the Elementary Education Act, 1876, or the Education (Scotland) Act, 1878, as amended by any later enactment

Employment in Mines.

The Mines (Prohibition of Child Labour Underground) Act, 1900, is now repealed, but its provisions are reproduced in the Coal Mines Act, 1911 [1] The limitations imposed by this Act are as follows—

"No boy under the age of fourteen years, and no girl or woman of any age shall be employed in or allowed to be for the purpose of employment in any mine below ground" This section applies to any underground workings.

The provisions as to working above ground [2] are more detailed and have the following effect—

"(1) No boy or girl under the age of thirteen shall be so employed, unless lawfully so employed before the passing of this Act;

---

[1] 1 and 2 Geo V, Ch. 50, Secs 91, 92   [2] Sec 92

"(2) No boy or girl of, or above, the age of thirteen years and no woman shall be employed for more than fifty-four hours in any one week, or more than ten hours in any one day;

"(3) No boy, girl, or woman shall be so employed between the hours of nine at night and five on the following morning, nor on Sunday, nor after two o'clock on Saturday afternoons;

"(4) There shall be an interval of not less than twelve hours between the termination of employment on one day and the commencement of the next employment;

"(5) A week shall be deemed to begin at midnight on Saturday night and to end at midnight on the succeeding Saturday night;

"(6) No boy, girl, or woman shall be employed continuously for more than five hours without an interval of at least half an hour for a meal, nor for more than eight hours on any one day without an interval or intervals for meals amounting altogether to not less than one hour and a half;

"(7) No boy, girl, or woman shall be employed in moving railway waggons, or in lifting, carrying, or moving anything so heavy as to be likely to cause injury to the boy, girl, or woman;[1]

"(8) The term 'boy' means a male under sixteen, and the term 'girl' means a female under sixteen."[2]

A period of employment and time allowance for meals is to be fixed within the foregoing limits by the manager. No change can be made in the times fixed more often than once quarterly without written consent from an Inspector of Mines unless some special cause is shown

A register of boys, girls, and women employed above ground and of boys below ground is to be kept by the owner, agent, or manager of the mine. This register, in the form prescribed by the Home Secretary, must show the name, age, residence, and date of first employment of such persons. It is open to inspection by any Inspector of Mines and by any officer of the local authority for the area in which the mine is situate. Failure to comply with the terms of the Act is an offence which may be prosecuted in the manner directed by the Summary Jurisdiction Acts subject to an appeal to quarter sessions in cases within section 104 of the Act.[3]

Young Persons Under Eighteen.

Although as a rule the limit of legislative interference with hours

---

[1] See Employment of Children Act, 1903, for general provision on this point, p 125
[2] Sec. 122
[3] 1 and 2 Geo V, Ch 50, Secs 103, 104

of labour in the case of males is sixteen years, the Shops Act, 1912,[1] raises this limit to eighteen years. It is provided[2] that no person under the age of eighteen shall be employed in or about a shop for a longer period than seventy-four hours, including meals, in any week. Further, no young person, that is, no person under eighteen shall be employed in or about a shop after having previously been employed in a factory or workshop for the number of hours permitted by the Factory and Workshop Act, 1901, or for a longer period than will, together with the time during which he has been previously employed on the same day in a factory or workshop, complete such number of hours

Where young persons as above defined are employed in shops, it is necessary for the occupier to keep exhibited a notice specifying the number of hours in the week during which a young person may be lawfully employed and referring to the section[3] of the Shops Act which makes the provision

The penalty for employing young persons contrary to the Act is £1 for each person so employed and the penalty for failing to exhibit the notice in a conspicuous place is not to exceed 40s The Act does not apply to domestic servants, but it applies to assistants in wholesale shops and warehouses although the term "shop" as generally used in the Act means any premises where a retail trade or business is carried on including barbers, hairdressers, and refreshment houses Programme-sellers at theatres and places of amusement are not shop assistants nor are persons assisting at any fair lawfully held or any bazaar or sale of work for charitable or other purposes from which no private profit is derived [4]

Certain limitations are laid down[5] in the Act in respect of its application to rural districts in Ireland.

Dangerous Performances

In order to protect children and young persons from the effects of dangerous performances two Acts[6] have been passed The joint effect of these Acts is to prohibit any person from causing a child under fourteen, or young person, if a male under sixteen, if a female

---

[1] 2 Geo V, Ch 3   [2] Sec 2   [3] Sec 2
[4] Sec 19   [5] Sec 21 and Schedule 4
[6] Children (Dangerous Performances) Act, 42 and 43 Vict, Ch 34, and Dangerous Performances Act, 1897, 60 and 61 Vict., Ch 52

under eighteen, to take part in a public exhibition or performance whereby in the opinion of a Court of summary jurisdiction the life or limbs of such child or young person shall be endangered. The parent or guardian or any person having the custody of such child is also subject to penalties if he aids or abets such person. The penalty inflicted upon either the person causing the child to perform or the parent or guardian of the child is fixed at a maximum of £10

Where, in the course of a public exhibition of a performance which is dangerous to life or limb, any accident causing actual bodily harm occurs to a child or young person, the employer is liable to be indicted as for an assault, and in addition the Court may award compensation not exceeding £20 to be paid by the employer to the child or to some person on the child's behalf. A prosecution may not be instituted without the consent in writing of the chief of the police of the area in which the offence is committed unless an accident has actually happened, causing injury to the child or young person

Assistance in Child Employment

The main provision regulating the employment of children and young persons in various businesses and circumstances having been noted, it may be well to indicate a new departure[1] which the legislature has seen fit to provide in order that children and young persons on leaving school may be more beneficially employed than in the past, and that some attempt may be made to bring an end to the economic waste due to the entry of young people into *cul de sac* employments.

Education Act, 1902.

Very wide powers are given to local education authorities to take such steps as seem to them desirable after consulting with the Board of Education, to supply or aid the supply of higher education, and to promote the general co-ordination of all forms of education The Education (Choice of Employment) Act, 1910,[2] extends the interpretation of this provision to include a power

---
[1] The Education (Choice of Employment) Act, 1910
[2] 10 Ed. VII, and 1 Geo V, Ch 37.

to make arrangements, subject to the approval of the Board of Education, for giving to boys and girls under seventeen years of age assistance with respect to the choice of suitable employments, by means of the collection and the communication of information and the furnishing of advice This power has already been taken advantage of and is being exercised in our large cities in conjunction with the labour exchanges and bureaux

INDEX

ABANDONMENT and exposure, 21
Absence of child, Court acts in, 35
Accident during dangerous performance, 135
Age of child, presumption as to, 10, 17
——— ———, proof of, 17
Age of young person, presumed, 17
Agent liable for employing contrary to Employment of Children Act, 126
Appeal to Quarter Sessions in cruelty cases, 36
Assaults, ill-treats, neglects, 20
Authority of constable or park-keeper (tobacco), 4
——— ——— parent to punish, 19
——— ——— assistant schoolmaster, 19
——— ——— schoolmaster, 19
Automatic machines and juvenile smoking, 4
Auxiliary homes, 92
Avoidance of insurance policy, 42

BAR, definition, 6
———, exclusion of children from, 6
Begging, 7
Betting with infants, 8
——— ——— ——— in the street, 9
Bibliography, xix et seq
Board of Guardians as parent, 83
Boarding-out children from industrial schools, 93
By-laws as to street trading, 124
——— ——— under Employment of Children Act, 125
——— ——— under Education Acts, 78

CARE of child, temporary order, 26
——— ———, meaning of, 16
Certificate of age, for employment, 119
——— ———, falsely given, 126
Charity, conditions as to employment do not apply to, 130
Children (Employment Abroad) Act, 1913, 12
Child, definition, 15, 90, 129
——— in company of reputed thief, 95

Child without settled place of abode, 95
Choice of employment, assistance in, 135
Consul and children abroad, 13
Contribution towards maintenance by parents, 28, 111, 115
——— ——— ——— by Guardians, 109
Conveyancing Act, 1881, and maintenance, 59
Conveyance to industrial school, 99
Costs and expenses, 40, 43
Cleansing verminous children, 76
Cruelty, 15
———, amounting to manslaughter, 23
———, wilful, 18
Custody, charge, or care, defined, 16
———, order under Children Act, 17
———, order by Chancery Division, 55, 57
———, order under Employment of Children Act, 126
———, order by P D A Division, 53
——— of a relative, 26, 126

DANGEROUS performances, viii, 134
——— Performances Acts, 134
——— trades, vii, 125
Dates of acts of cruelty where several, 36
Day industrial schools, 113
Death of child cruelly treated, 23
——— ———, interest in, 22, 23
Depositions of a child, 33
———, admission of in evidence, 34
Destitute children, 95
Detention in a place of safety, 25
——— order, operation deferred, 98
Disposal of child in custody of fit person, 26, 126
Duties of local authorities in respect of industrial schools, 107

EDUCATION Authority and detention of child in industrial school, 108, 115
——— generally, 66 et seq
——— of blind children, 82
——— of deaf children, 82
——— of defective children, 84
——— of epileptic children, 84

137

Education of children in industrial schools, 90 *et seq*
—— of young persons in reformatories, 90 *et seq*
Emigration of child from industrial school, 104
Employ, definition of, 129
Employer, liable as for assault under Dangerous Performances Act, 135
—— may charge a workman under Employment of Children Act, 127
Employment of Children Act, 123
—— —— abroad, 12
—— —— in factories, 129
—— —— in mines, 132
—— offences, 116 *et seq*
—— licences, 131
—— in underground workings, 132
Escape from school, 105
—— whilst on licence from industrial school, 101
Evidence, copy of policy of insurance as, 23
—— of child on oath, 35
—— —— not on oath, 34
—— ——, when corroboration necessary, 35
—— of child by depositions, 34
—— of child's age, 68
—— of child, false, 35
—— of defendant, wife or husband, 33
Exclusion of children from bars, 6
—— —— —— —— Court, 2
—— of public from Court on trial of children, 2
—— —— verminous children from school, 75 *et seq*
Exemption from school attendance, 79, 117
Expenses of certified schools, contribution by Treasury, 106, 114
—— —— ——, how defrayed, 110
Exposing to risk of burning, 23

Factory Act, 119
—— ——, conflict with Education Acts, 119
—— ——, employer's liability under, 122
—— ——, partial exemption from attendance under, 120
—— ——, provisions extend to laundries, 122
Father's common law right to control his children, 50
Fine for administering intoxicants to children, 7

Fine for breach of Education Act as to attendance, 67
—— —— —— of employment, 118
—— —— —— of Employment of Children Act, 126
—— —— —— of Factory Act, employer, 122
—— —— —— ——, parent, 123
—— —— —— of Shops Act relating to young persons, 134
—— —— not excluding children from bars, 6
—— —— supplying intoxicants to children, 5
—— —— supplying smoking materials, 3
—— under Children Act for cruelty, 22
First offences and industrial schools, 96
Forfeiture of tobacco, 3
Flannelette danger, 24
French Law, x
—— Tribunal de l'Enfant, xii
—— Law of 22 July, 1912, xii

German Law, employment register, viii
—— ——, hours of employment, vii
—— ——, school leaving-age, vii
Giving access to child, 55
Guardian, parent, etc, 83
——, meaning under Employment of Children Act, 129
——, appointment of, 53, 56
——, duties of, 57
——, father as, 51
——, mother as, 53
——, removal of, 56
——, statutory, 56
——, testamentary, 56
—— and ward, Court's authority, 57
Guardians instituting proceedings, 36
—— —— not parent, 83, 84
Guardianship of Infants Act, 51

Habitual drunkard, parent, 32
—— ——, child of, sent to Industrial school, 95

Ill-treats, meaning of, 20
Industrial School, 90 *et seq*
—— ——, certification of, 91
—— ——, commitment to, 94
—— ——, day, 113

Industrial School, definition of, 90
—— ——, discharge from, 103
—— ——, escape from, 105
—— ——, expenses in, 106 et seq
—— ——, guardians' contributions to, 109
—— ——, inspection of, 91
—— ——, managers of, 92
—— ——, period of detention in, 99
—— —— provided by Education Authority, 108
—— —— reception under an attendance order, 114
—— ——, resignation of certificate of, 91
—— ——, Treasury contributions to, 114
—— ——, transfer from, 103
—— ——, withdrawal of certificate of, 91
—— ——, what children may be sent to, 94 et seq
Information on oath for search warrant, 30
Injury in school, 46 et seq
Inspector's powers, Children Act, 31, 39
—— —— Factory Act, 122 et seq
—— —— under Employment of Children Act, 131
Insurance on child's life, effect in cruelty cases, 23, 42
Intoxicants and children, sale of, 5
—— —— ——, giving, 7
Italian Law, xiii
—— Criminal Code, xiv, xvi
—— itinerant professions, xvi
—— labour in mines, xvii
—— Patronati perminorenni, xiv
—— Police Act, xviii

JUVENILE smoking, 3

LABOUR in mines, vii, 132
—— at night, vii, 124
Licences for employment of children, 124, 131
—— from Industrial schools, 101
—— under Children (Employment Abroad) Act, 131
Limit of time for proceedings under Children Act, 35
—— —— —— —— Employment of Children Act, 128
Loans to infants, 10
Local Authorities and expenses under Children Act, Part I, 40, 43

Local Authorities fix number of infants for reward, 41

MAINTENANCE of infants or young persons, 28, 58, 111, 115
——, parents' contribution towards, 28, 111, 115
Manslaughter, indictment for cruelty or, 23
Medical assistance, failure to provide, 21
—— certificate of fitness for labour, 119
—— —— intimating unsuitable occupation, 125
—— treatment, cost of, 88
Minimum working age in England, 118
—— —— —— in France, xi
—— —— —— in Germany, ix
—— —— —— in Spain, vi
—— —— —— in Italy, xvii
Mines, labour in, vi, xvi, 132
Moral welfare, 1 et seq

NEGLECT, definition, 20
Night labour, 124
—— —— in mines, 133
Notice to police by persons desiring to employ children, 132
—— —— by persons taking infants for reward, 38, 43
—— to coroner of infant's death, 42

OFFENCES of cruelty against children, 15
Offenders conditionally pardoned, 94
Order as to access, 55
—— for temporary custody, how made, 26
—— as to custody in Chancery Division, 55, 57
—— —— —— under Children Act, 27
—— —— —— Employment of Children Act, 126
—— —— —— in P D and A Division, 53
—— —— ——, variation of, 27
—— —— maintenance by Chancery Division, 58
—— —— —— under Children Act, 28
Overlaying, 22

PARENT, habitual drunkard, 32
—— has care and custody, 17

Parent, meaning of term, 83
Parents' authority limited, 102
——— liability for false certificate of age, 126
——— ———, for breach of Factory Acts, 123
——— ——— for contribution to child's maintenance, 28, 111, 115
——— ——— for child's education, 65 et seq.
——— ——— for education of defective child, 82 et seq
——— ——— for right to control religious education, 60
——— ——— to punish in proper case, 19
Parental authority granted to a fit person, 27
Pensions, attachment of, 29
Place of safety, detention in, 25
Police, and dangerous performances, 135
———, safety of children at entertainments, 44
———, notices as to infants taken for reward, 41
———, notice of intention to apply for licence, 132
Pawning by children, provisions against, 2
Power to clear Court during evidence of young persons, 2
——— ——— exclude children from Court, 2
——— ——— constables as to offences under Children Act, 25
Presumption of infancy, 8
——— ——— age, Betting and Loans Act, 9
——— ———, Moneylenders Act, 11
——— ———, Street Betting Act, 10
——— ——— of child, 18, 68
——— ——— of young person, 18
Prohibition against receiving children for reward, 41
Proof of age in cruelty cases, 16
——— ——— in employment, 119
Prosecution of offences under Part I, Children Act, 43
Provision of fireguards, 23
Punishment of children by parents, 19
——— ——— in school, 19
——— for not making safety provision at entertainments, 45
——— for offences of cruelty, 22, 43
——— ——— under Dangerous Performances Act, 135
——— ——— ——— Education Acts, 67

Punishment for offences under Employment Abroad Act, 13
——— ——— ——— ——— of Children Act, 126
——— ——— ——— Misdescription of Fabrics Act, 24
——— ——— ——— Mines Act, 133
——— ——— ——— Street Betting Act, 9
——— ——— ——— Shops Act, 134
——— ——— selling cigarettes to children, 3
REFORMATORY Schools, 90 et seq.
———, certification of, 90
———, commitment to, 93
———, definition of, 90
———, discharge from, 103
———, escape from, 105
———, expenses in, 106, 109
———, inspection of, 91
———, period of detention in, 99
——— provided by local authority, 109
———, resignation of certificate of, 91
———, transfer from, 103
———, withdrawal of certificate of, 91
———, who may be sent to, 93
Refractory children, 96, 97
Register of children and women employed in mines, 33
Relative, child committed to care of, 97
Religion of child safeguarded, 29, 100
Religio sequitur patrem, 62
Removal of infant improperly kept, 41
——— ——— warrant, 30
Respondeat superior in criminal cases, 11
Restrictions as to employment, 130
Risk of burning, 23

SAFETY of children at entertainments, 44
——— from fire, 23
Search warrant, 30
Selling smoking materials, 3
Seizing smoking materials, 3
Smoking by children, 3
Spanish Law, education ten to fourteen, vi
——— ——— to eighteen, vii
——— ———, mining and other dangerous work, vii
——— ———, night work, vii
Statutes referred to—
Stat 5 Eliz, Ch 2, 116

Statutes referred to—
5 Eliz., Ch. 4, 60
43 Eliz, Ch 2, 60
1 Jac. I, Ch. 4, 61
1 Jac I, Ch 25, 60, 116
3 Jac. I, Ch 5, 61, 116
7 Jac I, Ch. 3, 60
3 Car I, Ch 2, 61
8 & 9 Wm. & Mary, Ch 30, 60
11 & 12 Wm. III, Ch 4, 62
1 Anne, Statute I, Ch 30, 62
2 & 3 Anne, Ch. 6, 60
4 & 5 Anne, Ch 19, 60
17 Geo. II, Ch 5, 60
18 Geo III, Ch 47, 60
11 & 12 Vict, Ch 42
(Indictable Offences Act, 1848), 34
20 & 21 Vict Ch 85
(Matrimonial Causes Act, 1857), 54
22 & 23 Vict Ch. 61
(Matrimonial Causes Act, 1859), 54
24 & 25 Vict Ch 100
(Offences against the Person Act, 1861), 21
33 & 34 Vict Ch 75
(Elem Education Act, 1870), 65 et seq
34 & 35 Vict Ch 112, 2
35 & 36 Vict Ch 93
(Pawnbrokers Act, 1872), 3
36 & 37 Vict, Ch 12
(Custody of Infants Act, 1873), 51, 57
36 & 37 Vict Ch 86
(Elem Education Act, 1873), 68
37 & 38 Vict, Ch 62
(Infants Relief Act, 1874), 10
39 & 40 Vict Ch 79
(Education Act, 1876), 68 et seq
42 & 43 Vict Ch 19
(Inebriates Act, 1879), 33
42 & 43 Vict Ch 34
(Dangerous Performances Act, 1879), 25, 134
42 & 43 Vict Ch 49
(Summary Jurisdiction Act, 1879), 22
43 & 44 Vict Ch 23
(Elem Education Act, 1880), 65, 70
44 & 45 Vict Ch 41
(Conveyancing Act, 1881), 58
47 & 48 Vict Ch 68
(Matrimonial Causes Act, 1884), 54

Statutes referred to—
48 & 49 Vict., Ch. 69
(Criminal Law Amendment Act, 1885), 25
49 & 50 Vict Ch 27
(Guardianship of Infants Act, 1886), 51 et seq.
54 & 55 Vict Ch 39
(Factory Act, 1891), 120
55 & 56 Vict Ch 4
(Betting and Loans [Infants] Act, 1892), 8
56 & 57 Vict Ch 42
(Elem Education Act, 1893), 65
57 & 58 Vict. Ch. 41
(Prevention of Cruelty to Children Act, 1894), 15, 33
57 & 58 Vict Ch 60, 2
58 & 59 Vict Ch. 39
(Summary Jurisdiction [Married Women] Act, 1895), 55
60 & 61 Vict Ch 52
(Dangerous Performances Act, 1897), 25, 134
61 & 62 Vict Ch 36
(Criminal Evidence Act, 1898), 33
62 & 63 Vict Ch 13
(Elem. Education Act [1893] Amendment Act, 1899), 117
62 & 63 Vict Ch 32
(Elem Education [Defective and Epileptic Children] Act, 1899), 84
63 & 64 Vict Ch 51
(Moneylenders Act, 1900), 11
63 & 64 Vict Ch 53
(Elem Education Act, 1900), 67, 117–119
1 Ed VII, Ch 22
(Factory and Workshop Act, 1901), 120
2 Ed VII, Ch 42
(Education Act, 1902), 46, 65 et seq
3 Ed VII, Ch 45
(Employment of Children Act, 1903), 50, 123 et seq
4 Ed VII, Ch 15
(Prevention of Cruelty to Children Act, 1904), 15
6 Ed VII, Ch 43
(Street Betting Act, 1906), 9
6 Ed VII, Ch 57
(Education [Provision of Meals] Act, 1906), 86
7 Ed VII, Ch 17
(Probation of Offenders Act, 1907), 96

Statutes referred to—
  7 Ed VII, Ch 40
    (Notification of Births Act, 1907), 38
  7 Ed VII, Ch 43
    (Education [Administrative Provisions] Act, 1907), 46, 66, 69, 85, 110
  8 Ed VII, Ch 57
    (Children Act, 1908), 1-46, 90 et seq
  9 Ed VII, Ch 13
    (Local Education Authorities [Medical Treatment] Act, 1909, 88
  10 Ed VII & 1 Geo V, Ch 24
    (Licensing [Consolidation] Act, 1910), 5
  10 Ed VII & 1 Geo V, Ch 37
    (Education [Choice of Employment] Act, 1910), 135
  1 & 2 Geo V, Ch 32
    (Education [Administrative Provisions] Act, 1911), 89
  1 & 2 Geo V, Ch 50
    (Coal Mines Act, 1911), 128, 132
  2 Geo V, Ch. 3
    (Shops Act, 1912), 134
  3 & 4 Geo V, Ch 7
    (Children [Employment Abroad] Act, 1913), 13, 25
  3 & 4 Geo V, Ch 17
    (Fabrics [Misdescription] Act, 1913), 24

Statutes referred to—
  4 & 5 Geo, V, Ch. 20
    (Education [Provision of Meals] Act, 1914), 87
  4 & 5 Geo V, Ch 58
    (Criminal Law Administration Act, 1914), 115
Street trading, 124
Suffering not to be proved in cruelty cases, 18
Suffocation of infants by overlaying, 22

TAKING into employment, 123
Teacher's liability for injury to child, 48
—— right to punish, 19
—— ——, how excluded, 19
Temporary order for custody of child, 26
Tobacco, selling to children, 3
——, forfeiture of, 3
——, what young person may purchase, 4

UNDUE influence, 12

VISITATION of houses for reception of children, 31

YOUNG person, definition, 15
—— ——, under Shops Act, 133
—— ——, under supervision, 98
Youthful delinquent, 115
—— offender, 93

THE END

Pitman's
Business Handbooks

A Selected List of Practical Guides for Business Men and Advanced Students

CONTENTS

	PAGE		PAGE
ADVERTISING AS A BUSINESS FORCE	15	INCOME TAX PRACTICE	9
ADS AND SALES	15	INCOME TAX LAW	12
ACCOUNTS OF EXECUTORS	10	INSURANCE	4
ACCOUNTANCY	9	INSURANCE OFFICE ORGANISATION, ETC	4
AUDITING, ACCOUNTING, AND BANKING	6		
BALANCE SHEETS	7	LAW RELATING TO SECRET COMMISSIONS, ETC	12
BANK ORGANISATION, MANAGEMENT AND ACCOUNTS	5	LAW OF EVIDENCE	13
BANKRUPTCY AND BILLS OF SALE	10	LAW OF REPAIRS	13
BILLS, CHEQUES, AND NOTES	7	LICENSING, GUIDE TO THE LAW OF	11
BOOK-KEEPING, DICTIONARY OF	8	LECTURES ON BRITISH COMMERCE	3
BUSINESS MAN'S GUIDE	2	LOCAL GOVERNMENT CASE LAW	11
CARRIAGE, LAW OF	12	MANUFACTURING BOOK KEEPING AND COSTS	9
CHAIRMAN'S MANUAL	4		
CLUBS AND THEIR MANAGEMENT	3	MARINE LAW	11
"COTT" CODE DICTIONARY	16	MERCANTILE LAW	11
COLLIERY OFFICE ORGANISATION	6	MONEY, EXCHANGE, AND BANKING	6
COMPANY ACCOUNTS	9	OFFICE ORGANISATION	4
COMMERCIAL ENCYCLOPÆDIA	2	OUTLINES OF THE ECONOMIC HISTORY OF ENGLAND	16
COMPANIES AND COMPANY LAW	12		
COMPANY CASE LAW	12	PERSONAL ACCOUNTS	10
CONSULAR REQUIREMENTS	14	PRINCIPLES OF PRACTICAL PUBLICITY	15
COST ACCOUNTS	9	PRACTICAL BANKING	7
COUNTING HOUSE AND FACTORY ORGANISATION	4	PRACTICAL SALESMANSHIP	15
		PROSPECTUSES	7
DICTIONARY OF BANKING	6	PUBLIC MAN'S GUIDE	3
DICTIONARY OF COMMERCIAL CORRESPONDENCE	14	PSYCHOLOGY OF ADVERTISING	14
		RAILWAY ACCOUNTS	10
DICTIONARY, PORTUGUESE AND ENGLISH	13	RAILWAY REBATES CASE LAW	11
		SECRETARY'S HANDBOOK	7
DICTIONARY (ABRIDGED), PORTUGUESE AND ENGLISH	14	SHIPPING OFFICE ORGANISATION, ETC	5
		SOLICITOR'S OFFICE ORGANISATION, ETC	5
DICTIONARY OF SECRETARIAL LAW	8		
DICTIONARY OF THE WORLD'S COMMERCIAL PRODUCTS	13	STOCK EXCHANGE	10
		STOCK-BROKER'S OFFICE ORGANISATION	6
DRAPERY BUSINESS ORGANISATION	5		
ECONOMIC GEOGRAPHY	16	SYSTEMATIC INDEXING	15
ECONOMICS FOR BUSINESS MEN	16	TELEGRAPH CIPHERS	15
FARM ACCOUNTS	10	TRAMWAY RATING VALUATIONS	16
GROCERY BUSINESS ORGANISATION	5	TRANSFER OF STOCKS AND SHARES	8
GOLD MINE ACCOUNTS	9	THEORY AND PRACTICE OF ADVERTISING	14
GUIDE FOR THE COMPANY SECRETARY	7		
HANDBOOK OF LOCAL GOVERNMENT LAW	11	THEORY AND PRACTICE OF COMMERCE	13
HOUSEHOLD LAW	12	WORLD'S COMMERCIAL PRODUCTS	13

LONDON
SIR ISAAC PITMAN & SONS LTD, 1 AMEN CORNER, E C
BATH, NEW YORK AND MELBOURNE

Pitman's Complete List of Commercial Books post free on application

PITMAN'S COMMERCIAL ENCYCLOPÆDIA AND DICTIONARY OF BUSINESS. A reliable and comprehensive work of reference on all commercial subjects, specially designed and written for the busy merchant, the commercial student, and the modern man of affairs. Edited by J. A. SLATER, B.A., LL.B. (Lond.) Of the Middle Temple and North-Eastern Circuit Barrister-at-Law. Author of "Mercantile Law," "Commercial Law," etc., etc. Assisted by upwards of 50 specialists as contributors, including: W. Valentine Ball, M.A.; James O. Cheetham, B.Com.; Sidney W. Clarke; Arthur Coles, A.C.I.S.; A. C. Connell, LL.B. (Lond.); Emil Davies; Frank Dowler; J. Alfred Eke; J. B. Eland; R. A. Fletcher; A. J. Lawford Jones; G. H. Knott, M.A.; Samuel Moses, M.A.; W. Nicklin, A.S.A.A.; E. Martin, F.C.I.S.; E. J. Orford, F.R.G.S.; Gurdon Palin; H. W. Pointt; Harold Roberts, LL.B. (Lond.); W. P. Rutter, M.Com.; W. Courtney Sandford, B.A.; J. A. Slater, B.A., LL.B. (Lond.); W. E. Snelling; W. H. Spurr, A.C.I.S.; J. E. R. Stephens, B.A.; J. Wells Thatcher; P. Tovey, F.C.I.S.; A. R. Webb, A.S.A.A., A.C.A.; W. Jayne Weston, M.A., B.Sc. (Lond.). With numerous maps, illustrations, facsimile business forms and legal documents, diagrams, etc. In 4 vols., large crown 4to, (each 450 pp.,) cloth gilt, £1 10s. net. Half-leather gilt £2 2s. net.

"We have found it of an extremely interesting nature, and can strongly recommend it to all wishing to keep thoroughly up to date in commercial and business life. The high standard which Messrs. Pitman have attained in previous volumes published by them is fully sustained in the Commercial Encyclopædia, a strong feature of which is the extremely low price fixed for what may be regarded as a very important work of reference."—*The Statist*

"Providing, within adequate limits, full and accurate information upon every subject which can be legitimately claimed to fall within the scope of business life, this new work must appeal with peculiar force to all classes of the commercial community . . . should prove a more valuable possession to the business man than half-a-dozen dead languages and all the book-lore of 3,000 years."—*The Standard*

PITMAN'S BUSINESS MAN'S GUIDE. Sixth Revised Edition. With French, German, and Spanish equivalents for the Commercial Words and Terms. Edited by J. A. SLATER, B.A., LL.B. (Lond.), of the Middle Temple, Barrister-at-Law, and author of "The Commercial Law of England." The "Business Man's Guide" is a volume of handy size, designed to be of permanent usefulness in the office of the merchant, the banker, the broker, and the trader, and to all members of the staff from the manager, secretary, or cashier, to clerks of all kinds. The information is of such a character as will assist a business man in an emergency, and will clear up doubts and difficulties of every-day occurrence. The work includes over 2,000 articles. In crown 8vo, cloth gilt, 520 pp. 3s 6d net.

"An admirable specimen of the new type of business instruction book In 500 closely printed pages, with subjects arranged alphabetically, it packs away a great amount of information of the kind frequently required and not easily obtained by business men of many kinds. The fulness of the technical phraseology, with foreign equivalents, is one of the best features of the book. One may search any ordinary dictionary in vain for explanations of such phrases as 'bottomry bond,' 'hypothec,' 'quintal,' or 'fittage.' The summarised information of trade customs, of foreign practice, and of commercial law, is given with great lucidity. Altogether it is a book that can be heartily recommended."—*Daily Mail*

PITMAN'S PUBLIC MAN'S GUIDE. A Handbook for all who take an interest in questions of the day. Edited by J. A. SLATER, B A, LL B. (Lond.) The object of this book is to enable its readers to find within a comparatively compact compass information on any subject which can possibly bear upon matters political, diplomatic, municipal, or imperial. In crown 8vo, 444 pp, cloth gilt, 3s 6d. net.

"Comprehensive and concise are the two adjectives which best describe the 'Public Man's Guide,' to which might be added indispensable."—*Westminster Gazette.*
"Such a volume is this, giving a great mass of carefully selected and condensed information on a wide range of subjects, is exactly what is needed. The volume is, in fact, a miniature encyclopædia, not for the student, but for most general readers—one might say for 'the man in the street.'"—*Glasgow Evening News.*

LECTURES ON BRITISH COMMERCE, including Finance, Insurance, Business and Industry. By the Rt HON. FREDERICK HUTH JACKSON, G ARMITAGE-SMITH, M A., D.Litt., ROBERT BRUCE, C.B., DOUGLAS OWEN, W. E BARLING, J. J. BISGOOD, B A, ALLAN GREENWELL, F.G S, JAMES GRAHAM With a Preface by the HON W. PEMBER REEVES In demy 8vo, cloth gilt, 295 pp, 7s. 6d net.

CONTENTS —The Bank of England—The British System of Taxation—The London Postal Service London as a Port—The Machinery of Marine Insurance—British Shipping Fire Assurance, Life Assurance—Industrial Life Assurance, Personal Accident and Sickness Insurance, Workmen's Compensation Assurance, Motor Car Insurance, Burglary Assurance, etc.—The Economic Position of the Coal Industry of the United Kingdom—The Woollen Industry.

CLUBS AND THEIR MANAGEMENT. By FRANCIS W PIXLEY, F C A, of the Middle Temple, Barrister-at-Law In demy 8vo, cloth gilt, 240 pp, 7s 6d net.

The author of this book, who for some twelve years was on the committee of one of the leading London Clubs, is a past President of the Institute of Chartered Accountants, and Auditor of a number of Club and Hotel Accounts. It is believed that the work will appeal not only to members of Club Committees and Secretaries, but to Members of Clubs in England, in our oversea Dominions, and in America. It has nothing to do with the history of Clubs but with their practical management, and contains in detail the duties of every official of a Club from the Members of the Committee to the Hall Porter. Forms of accounts, specimen rules and by-laws, and a vast amount of general information help to complete the volume

THE CHAIRMAN'S MANUAL. Being a guide to the management of meetings in general, and of meetings of local authorities, with separate and complete treatment of the meetings of public companies. By GURDON PALIN, of Gray's Inn, Barrister-at-Law, and ERNEST MARTIN, F.C.I.S. In crown 8vo, cloth gilt, 192 pp., 2s. 6d. net.

"We only wish that it were a *sine quâ non* that no chairman should be allowed to occupy that position unless he could show that he had carefully perused this little book. We strongly urge all our readers to obtain a copy."—*Accountant's Journal*

INSURANCE. A Practical Exposition for the Student and Business Man. By T. E. YOUNG, B.A., F.R.A.S., ex-President of the Institute of Actuaries. Second Edition, Revised. In demy 8vo, cloth gilt, 408 pp. 5s. net.

"It is enough to say of the second edition of this well-known work that it retains all the valuable features of the first edition, and includes additional information of an important character. In particular the chapters upon fire, marine, and accident insurance have, on the invitation of Mr. Young, had the advantage of revision and approval by several well known experts in these departments. We can cordially commend this work to all students of insurance."—*Local Government Journal*

INSURANCE OFFICE ORGANISATION, MANAGEMENT, AND ACCOUNTS. By T. E. YOUNG, B.A., F.R.A.S., and RICHARD MASTERS, A.C.A. Second Edition, Revised. In demy 8vo, cloth gilt, 150 pp., 3s. 6d. net.

"The need of a suitable text book, dealing in a clear and comprehensive manner with the various aspects of life assurance both from the theoretical and the practical standpoint, has probably been felt by every student of this great branch of finance. A text-book admirably adapted to supply this want has now been prepared by Mr. T. E. Young. His long and varied experience as a practical manager and actuary, and his intimate associations for years with actuarial students have rendered him eminently qualified for undertaking such a work."—*The Insurance and Finance Chronicle*

OFFICE ORGANISATION AND MANAGEMENT. Including Secretarial Work. By LAWRENCE R. DICKSEE, M.Com., F.C.A., and H. E. BLAIN, Late Tramways Manager, County Borough of West Ham. In demy 8vo, cloth gilt, 306 pp., 5s. net.

"We have scarcely ever seen an office manual so complete and reliable as this one. The chapters on office management are compact with useful information, the ripe fruit of experience."—*Manchester City News*

"An enormous amount of useful information is comprised in the 300 pages of which the work consists."—*Accountant*.

COUNTING HOUSE AND FACTORY ORGANISATION. A Practical Manual of Modern Methods applied to the Counting House and Factory. By J. GILMOUR WILLIAMSON, *Holder of Business Diploma of the Heriot-Watt College, Edinburgh, etc.* In demy 8vo, cloth gilt, 182 pp., 5s. net.

"The volume deals exhaustively with the subject from all aspects, in some seventeen chapters, and discusses the work of the various departments of a business house from a practical standpoint. Theories are rightly eschewed. The work will undoubtedly receive a welcome from manufacturers who are aiming at efficiency, and who are anxious to inaugurate system or reorganise on reliable and tried lines, and there are doubtless not a few who are on the look out for a comprehensive volume containing practical hints."—*Hardware Trade Journal*

SHIPPING OFFICE ORGANISATION, MANAGEMENT, AND ACCOUNTS. A comprehensive Guide to the innumerable details connected with the Shipping Trade. By ALFRED CALVERT. In demy 8vo, cloth gilt, 203 pp., with numerous forms, 5s. net.

"This is the most practical handbook on the subject that we have seen. It is in the presentation line by line, in any part of the book, of the subject-matter treated, that the author shows his complete and intimate knowledge of the practice of the shipping trade. There is nothing dead or too theoretic about Mr. Calvert's book, and his method of explanation is eminently clear and forcible. We can confidently recommend the work. The book fully answers and makes good its title."—*Manchester Guardian.*

SOLICITOR'S OFFICE ORGANISATION, MANAGEMENT, AND ACCOUNTS. By E. A. COPE and H. W. H. ROBINS. In demy 8vo, cloth gilt, with numerous forms, 5s. net.

"The volume is rendered complete by the publication of numerous forms and diagrams, and the authors are to be congratulated on the thoroughness with which they have performed their task. We have no doubt whatever that the book will be extremely useful to the parties for whom it is intended."—*Birmingham Chamber of Commerce Journal.*

GROCERY BUSINESS ORGANISATION AND MANAGEMENT. By C. L. T. BEECHING, *Organising Secretary of the Institute of Certificated Grocers.* With Chapters on Buying a Business, Grocers' Office Work and Book-keeping, and a Model set of Grocers' Accounts. By J. ARTHUR SMART. In demy 8vo, cloth gilt, about 160 pp., with illustrations, 5s. net.

"The authors can speak with authority of the things of which they write, and they give us of their best. The book has twenty chapters, the topics of which extend from 'buying a business' to 'trading results.' Mr. Smart deals fully with the grocer's office work and book-keeping, and gives an admirable set of grocer's accounts . . . the work is well done throughout . . . it will be read with profit and pleasure."—*Grocer.*

DRAPERY BUSINESS ORGANISATION AND MANAGEMENT. By J. ERNEST BAYLEY. In demy 8vo, cloth gilt, 300 pp., 5s. net.

"The author has evidently spared no pains to make his work interesting, and in this he has so well succeeded that it can be read with advantage by both beginners and experts in the dry goods trade."—*Financial Times.*

BANK ORGANISATION, MANAGEMENT, AND ACCOUNTS. By J. F. DAVIS, D.Lit., M.A., LL.B. (Lond.) Lecturer in Banking and Finance at the City of London College. In demy 8vo, cloth gilt, with forms, 5s. net.

"It is concisely and clearly written, and the many examples of rulings of books and specimens of vouchers and forms in use form admirable illustrations to the text. The work should fulfil a useful purpose in providing the general survey of banking which has hitherto been lacking."—*Financial Times.*

STOCKBROKER'S OFFICE ORGANISATION, MANAGEMENT AND ACCOUNTS. By JULIUS E. DAY, Manager to an Inside Firm of Stockbrokers on the London Stock Exchange. In demy 8vo, cloth gilt, 243 pp., 7s. 6d. net.

"Without doubt there is a distinct need for this book, for it deals lucidly with many puzzling points of interest to the investor... The author is to be congratulated upon his achievement in grappling so successfully with a difficult task, for the book will prove an asset of considerable value to the beginner, and a work of undeniable interest to 'The man in Throgmorton Street.'"—*Joint Stock Companies' Journal.*

COLLIERY OFFICE ORGANISATION AND ACCOUNTS. By J. W. INNES, F.C.A. (Swithinbank Innes & Co., Chartered Accountants), and T. COLIN CAMPBELL, F.C.I., for many years Managing Clerk to a large Colliery Company, and now a principal Book-keeper at one of the largest Collieries in England. In demy 8vo, cloth gilt, 5s. net.

"This is a very useful book. It provides a manual for officials in a colliery office as well as affording many hints to those engaged as merchants and factors in the merchanting and distribution of coal. The work is certainly one which should find a place on the bookshelves of all those who are engaged in colliery working. The present work is an attempt to deal with the subject by practical men, who are fully conversant with the subject on which they write."—*Iron and Coal Trades Review.*

MONEY, EXCHANGE, AND BANKING, in their Practical, Theoretical, and Legal Aspects. A complete Manual for Bank Officials, Business Men, and Students of Commerce. By H. T. EASTON, of the Union of London and Smith's Bank, Ltd., Associate of the Institute of Bankers. Second Edition, Revised. In demy 8vo, cloth gilt, 312 pp., 5s. net.

"Mr. Easton's book can be commended to every one desiring guidance and instruction in the mysteries of money and exchange, and the theory and practice of banking."—*Truth.*

DICTIONARY OF BANKING. A Complete Encyclopædia of Banking Law and Practice. By W. THOMSON, Bank Inspector. With a section on the Irish Land Laws in their relation to Banking, by LLOYD CHRISTIAN, Secretary to the Institute of Bankers in Ireland. In crown 4to, half-leather gilt, 563 pp., 21s. net.

"Since the publication some years ago of Sir Inglis Palgrave's famous 'Dictionary of Political Economy' we have been favoured with no work of reference so useful to bankers as the one which has just been compiled by Mr. Thomson. Mr. Thomson has succeeded in his object of compiling a work which shall be of use both to the banking student and to the practical banker who requires information in a hurry."—*Bankers' Magazine.*

AUDITING, ACCOUNTING AND BANKING. By FRANK DOWLER, A.C.A., and E. MARDINOR HARRIS, *Associate of the Institute of Bankers.* In demy 8vo, cloth gilt, 328 pp., 5s. net.

"An authoritative book of real practical value. Diagrams, figures and explanations make the auditing part quite clear. Also the author has referred where, necessary, to legal cases. The banking section is lucid and practical, being far clearer than in books which one remembers having studied. It should be in every business or banking library, and would be helpful as a text book for examinations."—*T P's Weekly.*

PRACTICAL BANKING. Including Currency. A Guide to Modern Banking Practice and the Principles of Currency. By J. F. G. BAGSHAW, Associate of the Institute of Bankers, and C. F. HANNAFORD, Associate of the Institute of Bankers, Examiner in Banking and Currency to the London Chamber of Commerce. In demy 8vo, cloth gilt, 333 pp. 5s. net.

"This work is intended as a guide to modern banking practice and the principles of currency, and should be of great value to students of banking affairs. At the same time the information supplied is so well arranged that the book will prove of great service to bank officials for matters of reference. Owing to its wide scope, this book is especially useful to those in banking offices who are in the early years of their career."—*Bankers' Magazine*.

PITMAN'S BILLS, CHEQUES, AND NOTES. A Handbook for Business Men and Lawyers. Together with the Bills of Exchange Act, 1882, and the Bills of Exchange (Crossed Cheques) Act, 1906. By J. A. SLATER, B.A., LL.B. (Lond.) Barrister-at-Law. In demy 8vo, cloth gilt, 206 pp., 2s. 6d. net.

PITMAN'S GUIDE FOR THE COMPANY SECRETARY. A Practical Manual and Work of Reference with regard to the Duties of a Secretary to a Joint Stock Company. By ARTHUR COLES, A.C.I.S. With Introduction by HERBERT E. BLAIN. New edition, enlarged, and thoroughly revised. In demy 8vo, cloth gilt, 432 pp., with 54 facsimile forms, 5s. net.

"The title is sufficiently explanatory of the contents, but the book constitutes a manual for reference by secretaries of joint stock companies. The work seems to include every branch of secretarial duty, and to be excellently well done."—*Money Market Review*.

COMPANY ACCOUNTS. By the same Author. (See page 9.)

THE COMPANY SECRETARY'S VADE MECUM. A Manual of information on matters relating to Limited Liability Companies, for Directors, Secretaries, etc. In fool-cap 8vo, cloth, 1s. 6d. net.

PITMAN'S SECRETARY'S HANDBOOK. A Practical Guide to the Work and Duties in connection with the Position of Secretary to a Member of Parliament, a Country Gentleman with a landed estate, a Charitable Institution, with a section devoted to the work of a Lady Secretary and a chapter dealing with Secretarial work in general. Edited by H. E. BLAIN. In demy 8vo, cloth gilt, 168 pp., 3s. 6d. net.

BALANCE SHEETS. How to Read and Understand Them. A Complete Guide for Investors, Business Men, Commercial Students, etc. By PHILIP TOVEY, F.C.I.S. With 26 inset balance sheets. In foolscap 8vo, cloth, 1s. net.

PROSPECTUSES. HOW TO READ AND UNDERSTAND THEM. By the same Author. In demy 8vo, cloth gilt, 1s. 6d. net.

PITMAN'S DICTIONARY OF SECRETARIAL LAW AND PRACTICE. A Comprehensive Encyclopædia of Information and Direction on all matters connected with the work of a Company Secretary. Fully illustrated with the necessary forms and documents. With Sections on special branches of Secretarial Work. Edited by PHILIP TOVEY, F.C.I.S. With contributions by nearly 40 eminent authorities on Company Law and Secretarial Practice, including: G. N. Barnes, M.P.; F. Gore-Browne, K.C., M.A.; A. Crew, F.C.I.S., J. P. Earnshaw, F.C.I.S., M. Webster Jenkinson, F.C.A.; F. W. Pixley, F.C.A. In one handsome volume, half leather gilt, gilt top, 774 pp., 25s. net.

This work makes a very wide appeal. It explains in detail the duties and liabilities of a Secretary from the inception of a Company until the completion of its winding up, should such a course be necessary. Each stage in the history of a Limited Company, whether it be private or public, is fully dealt with, every important decision in Company Law has been embodied in the text, and for the benefit of the close student a synopsis of the leading cases is given in a large number of instances. Promoters and Directors will find in the pages of this work much valuable and interesting information. Careful and accurate expositions of their legal position are given, and their duties and liabilities are fully defined. Accountants, Financiers, Shareholders, Managers, and Students of Commerce, and, indeed, all who are directly or indirectly interested in Limited Companies, may consult the Dictionary with confidence on all matters appertaining to Company Law and Administration. Other important branches of the profession have not been overlooked, and adequate treatment has been given to the duties and responsibilities of Private Secretaries, Lady Secretaries, Secretaries to Trade Unions, and other organisations.

THE TRANSFER OF STOCKS, SHARES, AND OTHER MARKETABLE SECURITIES. A manual of the law and practice. By F. D. HEAD, B.A. (Oxon) *Late Classical Exhibitioner of Queen's College, of Lincoln's Inn, Barrister-at-Law*. Second edition, revised and enlarged. In demy 8vo, cloth gilt, 220 pp., 5s. net.

"The practising secretary is to be congratulated on the addition to his working library of this excellent text-book on one of the most complicated and difficult subjects with which he has to deal. Admirable alike in design and execution, this exposition of the law and the practice relating to the transfer of securities in joint stock companies is a complete and reliable handbook on transfers, to which the secretary may turn with confidence in the expectation of finding all the difficulties of the subject dealt with, and not slurred over in the far too usual manner."—*The Secretary*.

PITMAN'S DICTIONARY OF BOOK-KEEPING. An entirely new and unique work for teachers, students and practitioners providing in dictionary form information and guidance upon any point in Book-keeping and Accountancy. By R. J. PORTERS, Book-keeping Master at Pitman's School. In demy 8vo, cloth gilt, with many facsimiles, 780 pp., 5s. net.

INCOME TAX PRACTICE. By W. E. SNELLING, of the Inland Revenue Department. In demy 8vo, cloth gilt, about 400 pp., 10s. 6d. net. [*In preparation*]

The aim of this book, which is in accordance with the provisions of the Finance Act, 1914, is to provide a lucid and complete guide to the *practice* of income tax. It opens with concisely stated rules for the preparation and adjustment of accounts for income tax purposes. Succeeding chapters deal with the average system and the circumstances in which it may be departed from, the preparation of returns (including those of single traders, firms and companies), assessments on lands and houses, repayment claims and supertax returns and assessments. Then follows an exhaustive *dictionary of income tax* extending to over 100,000 words, arranged under 400 headings such as Advertisements, Depreciation, Employees, Foreign Traders, Gratuities, Licensed Premises, Plantations, Syndicates, Window Fittings, etc. Matters both large and small on which business men, secretaries, accountants and other tax-payers may require guidance have been sought out, and there can be few difficulties to which carefully reasoned solutions may not be readily found. The exhaustive character of the work, its arrangement in dictionary form, and its specimen accounts and returns make it unique among books on the subject.

MANUFACTURING BOOK-KEEPING AND COSTS. By GEORGE JOHNSON, F.C.I.S. In demy 8vo, cloth gilt, 120 pp., 3s. 6d. net.

"This is a very valuable and practical work on the accounts and books that a manufacturing establishment should keep. The book is a very useful one we trust that it will receive a hearty and practical welcome."—*Commercial Review*

ACCOUNTANCY. By F. W. PIXLEY, F.C.A., of the Middle Temple, Barrister-at-Law, Ex-President of the Institute of Chartered Accountants. In demy 8vo, cloth gilt, 318 pp., 5s. net.

"The work constitutes a very successful attempt to treat accountancy on a scientific basis. The author gives valuable advice on the construction of books and statements of account. The work is of a practical nature, and should be of the greatest value and assistance to intending practitioners."—*Money Market Review* "A careful, practical treatise."—*Times.*

COST ACCOUNTS in Principle and Practice. By A. CLIFFORD RIDGWAY, A.C.A. In demy 8vo, cloth gilt, with 40 specially prepared forms, 3s. 6d. net.

"This treatise deals exhaustively with its subject, and discusses the questions involved from the point of view both of principle and practice. Manufacturers especially should find it of great service."—*Financial Times*

COMPANY ACCOUNTS. By ARTHUR COLES, A.C.I.S. With a Preface by CHARLES COMINS, F.C.A. In demy 8vo, cloth gilt, 320 pp., 5s. net.

"We think Mr. Coles' book is one which will find favour both with practitioners and students. Its clearness and conciseness are commendable, and the author's experience has enabled him to deal with company accounts from a practical as well as a theoretical point of view."—*Accountant*

GOLD MINE ACCOUNTS AND COSTING. A Practical Manual for Officials, Accountants, Book-keepers, etc. By G. W. TAIT (of the South African staff of a leading group of mines). In demy 8vo, cloth gilt, 93 pp., 5s. net.

"The author of this book has had many years' practical experience in account keeping on the mines in South Africa, and the method he sets out will be found of considerable use to those keeping accounts of mines of all classes and in all parts of the world."—*Capitalist.*

THE ACCOUNTS OF EXECUTORS, ADMINISTRATORS AND TRUSTEES. With a Summary of the Law in so far as it relates to Accounts. By WILLIAM B. PHILLIPS, A.C.A. (Hons. Inter. and Final), A.C.I.S., formerly Lecturer on the subject to the Manchester Evening School of Commerce and the Manchester Chartered Accountants' Students' Society. In demy 8vo, cloth gilt, 3s. 6d. net.

"The book is very readable, and contains much that is helpful. Those called upon to act as executors, particularly those dealing with estates under English jurisdiction, will find their duties set out very clearly. The various illustrations are clearly set out, and will also be found helpful both to the practitioner and the student." — *Accountants' Magazine*

PERSONAL ACCOUNTS. By W. G. DOWSLEY, B.A., Lecturer in Book-keeping on the Modern Side, St. Andrew's College, Grahamstown. Size 15½ in. × 9¾ in., half-leather, 106 pp., with interleaved blotting-paper, 6s. 6d. net.

FARM ACCOUNTS. By the same Author. Size 15½ in. by 9½ in., half leather, 106 pp., interleaved blotting-paper. 6s. 6d. net.

RAILWAY ACCOUNTS AND FINANCE. Railway Companies (Accounts and Returns) Act, 1911. By ALLEN E. NEWHOOK, A.K.C., Sometime Lecturer at the London School of Economics on the Railway Companies (Accounts and Returns) Bill, 1911; Chief Accountant to the London and South-Western Railway Company. In demy 8vo, cloth gilt, 148 pp., 5s. net.

"Mr. Newhook writes with inside knowledge of railways, and his exposition of the new Act should be of assistance to all connected with the administration of British railway companies." — *Financier*

THE HISTORY, LAW, AND PRACTICE OF THE STOCK EXCHANGE. By A. P. POLEY, B.A., of the Inner Temple and Midland Circuit, Barrister-at-Law; and F. H. CARRUTHERS GOULD, of the Stock Exchange. Second edition revised and brought up to date. In demy 8vo, cloth gilt, 348 pp. 5s. net.

"It is possible to hail with something more than merely passing gratitude on our part, and we trust also on the part of members of the Stock Exchange, a new edition of a work which, on its first appearance, met with a reception commensurate with its merits. . . . worth double the price the Publishers ask for it." — *Financier*

BANKRUPTCY, BILLS OF SALE, AND DEEDS OF ARRANGEMENT. By W. VALENTINE BALL, M.A., of Lincoln's Inn, and the North Eastern Circuit, Barrister-at-Law. In demy 8vo, cloth gilt, about 400 pp., 5s. net. New, revised, and enlarged edition.

"Mr. Ball has elucidated an abstruse subject so clearly that the non-expert may consult with understanding and profit, but he has also kept in view the special requirements of chartered accountants." — *Financier*

PITMAN'S MERCANTILE LAW. By J. A. Slater, B.A., LL.B. A practical exposition for law students, business men, and advanced classes in commercial colleges and schools. Second Edition, Revised. In demy 8vo, cloth gilt, 448 pp., 5s. net.

"We are not surprised that a second edition should have been called for. Business men will find it a book of reference which will provide them with the rules of law upon general subjects in a short and clear form, and the law student, too, will find it of considerable assistance."—*Law Times.*

PITMAN'S HANDBOOK OF LOCAL GOVERNMENT LAW. Specially designed for all engaged in the offices of Local Authorities in England and Wales, and for Public Men. By J. Wells Thatcher. Of the Middle Temple, Barrister-at-Law. In crown 8vo, cloth gilt, 250 pp., 3s. 6d. net.

LOCAL GOVERNMENT CASE LAW. By Randolph A. Glen, M.A., LL.B. (Cantab.), Barrister-at-Law, of the Middle Temple and Western Circuit. In three volumes. Vol. I (1910), 176 pp., demy 8vo, cloth gilt, 5s. net. Vol. II (1911), about 350 pp., demy 8vo, cloth gilt, 7s. 6d. net. Vol. III (1912), 356 pp., in demy 8vo, cloth gilt, 10s. net.

In these three volumes over 1,200 cases (English, Scottish, and Irish), decided in 1910, 1911 and 1912, are collected for the use of Clerks to Local Authorities, Members of the Legal Profession, Justices of the Peace, local authorities and other municipal workers.

ENCYCLOPÆDIA OF MARINE LAW. By Lawrence Duckworth, of the Middle Temple, Barrister-at-Law. Second Edition. Revised. In demy 8vo, cloth gilt, 386 pp., 5s. net.

"The object of this volume is to place before a shipowner or anyone connected with maritime commerce, in well digested form, the essence of the law and the full meaning of words connected therewith. The advantage of such lucid condensation of a library of books in a single volume will, we venture to believe, be appreciated by busy men of commerce."—*Shipping World.*

PITMAN'S GUIDE TO THE LAW OF LICENSING. The handbook for all Licence-holders. By J. Wells Thatcher, Barrister-at-Law. In demy 8vo, cloth gilt, 200 pp., 5s. net.

This guide has been specially written for the use of licence-holders. The various subjects are treated in alphabetical order, and will be found easy for instant reference. The alphabetical arrangement of the titles will be of service, both to "The Trade," and to the trained minds of the legal profession, for it gives a short and accurate summary of each subject of the law of licensing.

RAILWAY (REBATES) CASE LAW. By Geo. B. Lissenden, Author of "Railway Trader's Guide," etc., etc. In demy 8vo, cloth gilt, 450 pp., 10s. 6d. net.

"Mr. Lissenden has done a great service. Any satisfactory report of these complicated cases before the Railway and Canal Commission must necessarily go into considerable detail, and this book supplies it, thereby saving the inquirer much trouble and expense by concentrating them in one volume."—*Railway Gazette.*

HOUSEHOLD LAW. By J. A. SLATER, B.A., LL.B. (Lond.). In demy 8vo, cloth gilt, 316 pp., 5s. net.

"The scheme of this book is quite admirable. It covers almost every phase of a householder's existence, and continues it even to the winding up of his estate."—*Morning Post.*

COMPANIES AND COMPANY LAW. Together with the Companies (Consolidation) Act, 1908. By A. C. CONNELL, LL.B. (Lond.), of the Middle Temple, Barrister-at-Law. In demy 8vo, cloth gilt, 348 pp., 5s. net.

"The volume before us will afford great assistance to all persons who are at any time brought into contact with joint stock companies. The numerous points of company law will be found to be lucidly explained, and copies of all the more important forms are set out."—*Law Times.*

COMPANY CASE LAW. By F. D. HEAD, B.A. (Oxon.), Late Classical Exhibitioner of Queen's College; of Lincoln's Inn, Barrister-at-Law. In demy 8vo, cloth gilt, 7s. 6d. net.
[*In preparation*]

This book is a digest of leading company law cases designed for the use of directors, secretaries, and others interested or concerned in joint stock companies, to whom the recognised official Law Reports are not always available for reference, and who may appreciate a summary of important decisions. It will also be useful to candidates preparing for examinations in company law held by various professional bodies. The author has referred in each case to the original report and abstracted therefrom the salient facts, summarising the decisions and adding, where necessary, brief extracts from the judgments. The book also contains an indexed copy of the Companies Acts, 1908 and 1913, and the Forged Transfers Acts, 1891 and 1892.

THE LAW OF CARRIAGE. By J. E. R. STEPHENS, B.A. Of the Middle Temple, Barrister-at-Law. In demy 8vo, cloth gilt, 324 pp., 5s. net.

"It deals with the subject in a clear, concise manner, and should undoubtedly appeal to those persons for whom it is intended. Practically the whole of the cases on this branch of the law are referred to in the volume."—*Law Times.*

INCOME TAX AND INHABITED HOUSE DUTY LAW AND CASES. A Practical Exposition of the Law, for the use of Income Tax Officials, Solicitors, Accountants, etc. By W. E. SNELLING, of the Inland Revenue Department. New Edition brought up-to-date in complete accordance with the Finance Act of 1914. In demy 8vo, cloth gilt, about 400 pp., 10s. 6d. net. [*In preparation*]

"Mr Snelling has done his work as compiler extremely well. The numerous sections are models of clearness and brevity, while in most instances they are illustrated and supported by references to the decisions of high legal authorities upon the particular points concerned."—*Morning Post.*

THE LAW RELATING TO SECRET COMMISSIONS AND BRIBES (CHRISTMAS BOXES, GRATUITIES, TIPS, ETC.) THE PREVENTION OF CORRUPTION ACT, 1906. By ALBERT CREW, of Gray's Inn, and the South Eastern Circuit, Barrister-at-Law; Lee Prizeman of Gray's Inn; author of "A Synopsis of Mercantile Law," "Company Law," etc. In demy 8vo, cloth gilt, 5s. net.

"It is an admirable summary of the law before and after the passing of the Prevention of Corruption Act, 1906, with an excellent analysis of the Act and full reference to cases. It is a very good handbook of its kind. The exposition is clear and reference is easy."—*Westminster Gazette*.

THE LAW OF REPAIRS AND DILAPIDATIONS. By T. Cato Worsfold, M.A., LL.D. In crown 8vo, cloth gilt, 3s. 6d. net.

THE LAW OF EVIDENCE. By W. Nembhard Hibbert, LL.D. (Lond.), Barrister-at-Law of the Middle Temple. In crown 8vo, cloth gilt, 3s. 6d. net.

THE WORLD'S COMMERCIAL PRODUCTS. A descriptive account of the Economic Plants of the World and of their Commercial Uses. By W. G. Freeman, B.Sc., F.L.S., Superintendent, Colonial Economic Collections, Imperial Institute, London, and S. E. Chandler, D.Sc., F.L.S., Assistant, Colonial Economic Collections, Imperial Institute, London. With contributions by numerous Specialists. In demy 4to, cloth gilt, 400 pp., 420 illustrations from photographs and 12 coloured plates and maps, 10s. 6d. net.

DICTIONARY OF THE WORLD'S COMMERCIAL PRODUCTS. With Equivalents in French, German, and Spanish. Second Edition, Revised. In demy 8vo, cloth gilt, 164 pp., 2s. 6d.

THE THEORY AND PRACTICE OF COMMERCE. Being a Complete Guide to Methods and Machinery of Business. Edited by F. Heelis, F.C.I.S., Author of "How to Teach Business Training," "Questions and Answers in Business Training," etc. *Examiner in Business Training to the Lancashire and Cheshire Union of Institutes, the West Riding County Council, and the Midland Union of Institutes*. Assisted by Specialist Contributors. In demy 8vo, cloth gilt, 620 pp., with many facsimile forms, 4s. 6d. net. Also in 2 vols., each price 2s. 6d. net.

A NEW DICTIONARY OF THE PORTUGUESE AND ENGLISH LANGUAGES. Based on a manuscript of Julius Cornet, by H. Michaelis. In two Parts. First Part: Portuguese-English. Second Part: English-Portuguese. Colloquial, commercial, and industrial terms have been plentifully introduced throughout the book and irregularities in the formation of the plural and in the conjugation of verbs have been carefully noted. Second Edition. Two volumes, each 15s. net.

ABRIDGED DICTIONARY OF THE PORTUGUESE AND ENGLISH LANGUAGES. Including Technical Expressions of Commerce and Industry, of Science and Arts. By H. MICHAELIS In crown 8vo, cloth, 15s. net

The present Dictionary is an abridgment of the author's larger Portuguese and English Dictionary, its whole construction and principal features being the same as those of the larger work. In two Parts — I. Portuguese-English. English-Portuguese. Both Parts in one vol.

PITMAN'S DICTIONARY OF COMMERCIAL CORRESPONDENCE IN FRENCH, GERMAN, SPANISH AND ITALIAN. Second, Revised, and cheaper Edition. In demy 8vo, cloth, 502 pp., 5s. net.

"Nine hundred columns are occupied by the dictionary, and in an appendix of more than fifty pages we have specimen letters dealing with the most important phases of commercial life. They are practical models which can easily be adapted. Care has been taken throughout to give the student the essentials of a good style of commercial correspondence in a clear and helpful fashion, and as a work of reference the volume is invaluable."—*Manchester Courier.*

PITMAN'S MERCANTILE CORRESPONDENCE. A Collection of Actual Letters arranged in Groups illustrating modern mercantile methods, and forming models for the Foreign Correspondent. Five volumes. Each in crown 8vo, cloth gilt, 250 pp.

ENGLISH .. .. 2s. 6d.   ENGLISH-FRENCH .. 2s. 6d.
ENGLISH-GERMAN .. 2s. 6d.   ENGLISH-ITALIAN .. 3s. 0d.
ENGLISH-PORTUGUESE .. 3s. 6d.

CONSULAR REQUIREMENTS FOR EXPORTERS AND SHIPPERS TO ALL PARTS OF THE WORLD. By J. S. NOWERY. In crown 8vo, cloth. With exact copies of all forms of Consular Invoices. 2s. 6d. net.

THE THEORY AND PRACTICE OF ADVERTISING. By WALTER DILL SCOTT, Ph.D., Director of the Psychological Laboratory of North Western University, U.S.A. In large crown 8vo, cloth, with 61 illustrations, 240 pp., 6s. net.

The Author of this work has made advertising the study of his life and is acknowledged as one of the greatest authorities on the subject in the United States.

THE PSYCHOLOGY OF ADVERTISING. A Simple Exposition of the Principles of Psychology and their Relation to Successful Advertising. By the same Author. In large crown 8vo, cloth, with 67 illustrations, 282 pp., 6s. net.

In this book, Professor Dill Scott does not merely state principles and theorize upon them—he furnishes characteristic examples and appropriate illustrations in explanation and support of his views.

PITMAN'S BUSINESS HANDBOOKS

THE PRINCIPLES OF PRACTICAL PUBLICITY. "The Art of Advertising." By TRUMAN A. DE WEESE. In large crown 8vo, cloth, with 43 full-page illustrations, 266 pp., 7s. 6d. net.

The book will be found a comprehensive and practical treatise covering the subject in all its branches, showing the successful adaptation of advertising to all lines of business.

ADVERTISING AS A BUSINESS FORCE. A Compilation of Experience Records. By P. T. CHERINGTON, Instructor in Commercial Organisation in the Graduate School of Business Administration, Harvard University. In demy 8vo, cloth gilt, 586 pp., 7s. 6d. net.

"Prof. Cherington's book is incomparably the best and most authoritative work on the general subject of advertising that has yet been issued. Here, at last, we have a book that represents advertising in the way its most advanced exponents see it that illustrates it with instances drawn from the field of actual occurrences."—*Printers' Ink* (U.S.A.)

THE PRINCIPLES OF ADVERTISING ARRANGEMENT. By F. A. PARSONS, President of the New York School of Fine and Applied Art. Size 7 in. by 10½ in., cloth, 128 pp., with many illustrations. 6s. net.

PRACTICAL SALESMANSHIP. A treatise on the Art of Selling Goods. By N. C. FOWLER, Jnr. Assisted by twenty-nine Expert Salesmen, Sales managers, and prominent business men. In crown 8vo, cloth, 337 pp., 3s. 6d. net.

ADS AND SALES. A study of Advertising and Selling from the standpoint of the new principles of Scientific Management. By HERBERT N. CASSON. In demy 8vo, cloth, 6s. net.

SYSTEMATIC INDEXING. By J. KAISER. In royal 8vo, cloth gilt, with 32 illustrations and 12 coloured plates. 12s. 6d. net.

"Every bit of his book is worth reading; he not only shows what should be done, but why it should be done, and the reason that some other method should not be adopted. He gives very frequent illustrations to amplify his text, and a careful perusal of his views will enable the ordinary business man to quickly seize upon the essentials in useful indexing."—*Liverpool Journal of Commerce*

TELEGRAPH CIPHERS. By A. W. E. CROSFIELD, *A Municipal School of Commerce, Manchester.* Size, 12 in by 1_ cloth, 21s. net.

A condensed vocabulary of 101 Million pronounceable artificial words; letters, and with a difference of at least two letters between each half-wor letters.

THE "COLE" CODE, OR CODE DICTIONARY. Size 7¼ in. by 10 in., 272 pp., cloth. 15s. net.

This book contains a simple, safe, and economical method of cabling verbatim commercial, technical, and social messages, complete and up to date, with unlimited facilities for extensions to suit any kind of business, including cabling from books, catalogues, price lists, etc. There are also two extra vocabularies of 10,000,000 words each, arranged in alphabetical and numerical order.

ECONOMIC GEOGRAPHY. By J. McFarlane, M.A., M.Com., Lecturer in Geography in the University of Manchester. In demy 8vo, cloth gilt, 568 pp., with 18 illustrations, 7s. 6d. net.

This new and important work will appeal with special force to all those who have recognised the necessity of organising our teaching of commercial subjects on a more rational and scientific basis. Unfortunately for English students, it has long been considered that a mere enumeration of countries and towns, a scanty knowledge of exports and imports, and a scrappy acquaintance with what has been termed "Mathematical Geography," have been a sufficient equipment for the commercial side of schools. The modern English Universities have done much to dispel this idea, and the University of Manchester has taken no mean position in the advance which has been made. The author is a man of wide experience and most fully equipped for his task, and it is believed that the publication of his work will be the beginning of a new era in the teaching of the subject.

OUTLINES OF THE ECONOMIC HISTORY OF ENGLAND. A Study in Social Development. By H. O. Meredith, M.A., M.Com., Fellow of King's College, Cambridge; Professor of Economics, Queen's University, Belfast. In demy 8vo, cloth gilt, 376 pp., 5s. net.

"Beginning with the Economic development of Britain during the Roman occupation, the work traces the progress made down to the present day, in the course of which Mr Meredith discusses such interesting subjects as the genesis of capitalism, money and taxation, the growth of trade and industry, the trade union movement, the law and the wage earning classes, finance and national welfare, etc. To the student and busy man it affords an excellent introduction to the study of one of the most complex questions of the day."—*Chamber of Commerce Journal*.

ECONOMICS FOR BUSINESS MEN. By W. J. Weston, M.A. (Lond.), B.Sc. (Lond.). In crown 8vo, cloth, 1s. 6d. net.

COMMERCIAL TRAVELLING. A Guide to the Profession for present and prospective Salesmen "on the road." By Albert E. Bull. In crown 8vo, cloth gilt, 2s. 6d. net.

THE ECONOMICS OF TELEGRAPHS AND TELEPHONES. By John Lee, M.A., *Traffic Manager, Post Office Telegraphs*. In crown 8vo, cloth gilt, 2s. 6d. net.

TRAMWAY RATING VALUATIONS AND INCOME TAX ASSESSMENTS. By F. A. Mitcheson, *Accountant, Manchester Corporation Tramways*. In demy 8vo, cloth gilt, 2s. 6d. net.

Lightning Source UK Ltd.
Milton Keynes UK
UKHW031959050420
361356UK00010B/208